YOSEMITE
THE COMPLETE GUIDE

6th Edition

©2020 DESTINATION PRESS & ITS LICENSORS
ISBN: 978-1-940754-41-3

Written & Photographed
by James Kaiser

This book would not have been possible without the help of many generous people. Special thanks to Beth Pratt, Kenny Karst, Pete Divine, Bob Fry, Greg Stock, Greg Cox, Linda Eade, Chris Stein, Paul Rogers, Jean Redle, Josia Lamberto-Egan, Maria Matijasevic, Peter Bohler, Peter Brewitt, Cat Zusky, Bob & Mary Anderson, Karl Kahler, the Yosemite Conservancy, the staff at YNP, and everyone who spent time with me in the wilderness. Above all, special thanks to superstar ranger Dick Ewart, whose wisdom and humor have inspired thousands of visitors, including me.

As always, a very special thanks to my family, friends, and all the wonderful people I encountered while working on this guide.

All information in this guide has been exhaustively researched, but names, phone numbers, and other details do change. If you encounter a change or mistake while using this guide, please send an email to changes@jameskaiser.com. Your input will help make future editions of this guide even better.

Although every attempt has been made to ensure the accuracy of information contained within this guide, the author and publisher do not assume and disclaim any liability to any party for any loss or damage caused by errors or omissions. Information has been obtained from sources believed to be reliable, but its accuracy and completeness are not guaranteed. If the rigors and threats of nature are in any way beyond your capabilities, do not attempt any hike in this guide. Many photos contained within this guide depict people in precarious situations; do not assume that any situations depicted in this book are in any way safe. All maps in this guide are based on official USGS data, but serious hikers should supplement their outings with detailed hiking maps.

Printed in Singapore

YOSEMITE

• THE COMPLETE GUIDE •

6th Edition

Bestselling Yosemite Guidebook

NPD BookScan 2019

MIX
Paper from responsible sources
FSC® C005748
www.fsc.org

JAMES KAISER

CONGRATULATIONS!

If you've purchased this book, you're going to Yosemite. Perhaps you're already here. If so, you're in one of America's most extraordinary national parks—an alpine wonderland home to soaring cliffs, thundering waterfalls, and vast stretches of pristine wilderness. The Sierra Nevada Mountains contain some of America's most stunning scenery, and Yosemite is the crown jewel of the Sierra Nevada.

When I first started working on *Yosemite: The Complete Guide*, I thought it might take one year to complete. Three years later, the book was finished. There was so much to photograph—so much that changed from season to season—that one year, I quickly realized, could never do Yosemite justice. As I hiked the trails and wandered the backcountry, I became friends with some legendary rangers—men and women who had spent decades exploring the park. Over long talks by the campfire they imparted their love and knowledge of Yosemite to me. It's my goal to pass that wisdom on to you.

Yosemite is extraordinary, but it can also be overwhelming. You could easily spend a month here and not run out of things to do. But if you're like most people, you've only got a few days. Make those few days count! With a limited amount of time—and crowds that grow larger every year—you've got to plan your trip wisely. This book puts the best of Yosemite at your fingertips, helping you maximize your time for an unforgettable adventure. Whether you're here to hike, sight-see, or just relax and hang out, *Yosemite: The Complete Guide* is the only guidebook you'll need.

Now let me show you the best that Yosemite has to offer!

CONTENTS

ADVENTURES P.17

Hiking, backpacking, rock climbing, river rafting—Yosemite has it all. The only question is what not to do in the park!

BASICS P.32

Everything you need to know for a successful visit: entrance fees, lodging and camping, best times to visit—and how to deal with pesky black bears.

GEOLOGY P.41

Over the past 500 million years, Yosemite has been shaped by erupting volcanoes, Ice Age glaciers, massive rockfalls, and countless other splendid catastrophes.

ECOLOGY & WILDLIFE P.59

Yosemite's pristine mountain wilderness is home to thousands of fascinating plants and animals that coexist in remarkable ways. From miniature orchids to bighorn sheep, Yosemite's ecology is as stunning as its scenery.

HISTORY P.85

For centuries Yosemite Valley was home to the Ahwahneechee tribe. Following the Gold Rush, artists and adventurers discovered its charms. Yosemite later inspired visionaries like John Muir, Ansel Adams, and the rugged athletes who pioneered Big Wall rock climbing.

YOSEMITE VALLEY P.123

The most famous part of the park, home to soaring cliffs, towering granite domes, and six waterfalls over 1,000 feet tall. Discover what makes Yosemite Valley one of America's most beautiful destinations.

GLACIER POINT P.191

Three thousand feet above Yosemite Valley, Glacier Point offers panoramas of the park's most famous sights. Sunsets are spectacular, and clear nights provide some of the best stargazing in California.

TIOGA ROAD P.221

This 46-mile road rises into the heart of the High Sierra—a gorgeous alpine wilderness filled with shimmering lakes, snow-capped peaks, and some of the park's most dramatic scenery.

TUOLUMNE MEADOWS P.247

The largest high-altitude meadow in the Sierra Nevada is the jumping-off point for many of Yosemite's best hikes and backpacks.

WAWONA & HETCH HETCHY P.295, P.301

Wawona is home to the Mariposa Grove of Giant Sequoias, the largest sequoia grove in the park. Hetch Hetchy—once a beautiful valley, now a flooded reservoir—set the stage for one of America's earliest environmental battles.

YOSEMITE TOP 5

TOP 5 VIEWPOINTS

TOP 5 ADVENTURES

TOP 5 HIKES

TOP 5 WATERFALLS

Vernal Fall

Half Dome Cables

INTRODUCTION

NESTLED DEEP IN the heart of California's Sierra Nevada Mountains, Yosemite is one of America's most spectacular national parks. Its alpine scenery is bursting with superlatives: the highest waterfall in North America (Yosemite Falls), the most famous vertical rock face in the world (El Capitan), and the largest organisms of all time (giant sequoias). But no statistic can capture the park's staggering beauty. Yosemite's sheer cliffs and thundering waterfalls have inspired some of America's finest artists, and its remarkable scenery lures visitors from around the world.

Yosemite Valley is the crown jewel of the park. Just seven miles long by one mile wide, it represents less than 1% of the park's 1,200 square miles. But Yosemite Valley's sheer cliffs shelter some of the world's most dramatic sights: Half Dome, El Capitan, Yosemite Falls. Because Yosemite Valley is the most popular part of the park, it's home to most of the park's lodges and visitor facilities.

Above Yosemite Valley lies the High Sierra, a stunning alpine wilderness of shimmering lakes, snow-capped peaks, and miles of sparkling granite. Reached via Tioga Road—the only east/west road that crosses the entire park—the High Sierra is an outdoor paradise for hikers, backpackers and rock climbers. Tuolumne Meadows, which lies at an elevation of 8,600 feet, is the starting point for many spectacular hikes and backpacks.

Thirteen miles south of Yosemite Valley lies Wawona, a small village that provides quick access to the Mariposa Grove of Giant Sequoias, the largest of the park's three sequoia groves. Twenty miles north of Yosemite Valley lies Hetch Hetchy—once a beautiful valley, now a massive reservoir. Enormous waterfalls still tumble into the reservoir, but Hetch Hetchy is best known for the famous environmental battle it spawned a century ago.

Yosemite Valley was originally home to the Ahwahneechee tribe. Following the Gold Rush, adventurous artists sought out the remote landscape, and their dramatic paintings and photographs captivated audiences around the world. John Muir arrived in 1868, and his writings helped spur the creation of Yosemite National Park in 1890. In 1916 Ansel Adams first visited Yosemite, and in the 1930s alpinists pioneered advanced techniques that gave birth to the modern sport of rock climbing. Today Yosemite's breathtaking cliffs, peaks and waterfalls lure over four million visitors a year.

Yosemite Valley

Half Dome, Winter

Above Red Devil Lake

HIKING & BACKPACKING

THE SIERRA NEVADA has some of the best hiking in North America, and Yosemite has some of the best hiking in the Sierra Nevada. Over 800 miles of trails crisscross the park, ranging from easy day hikes to rugged multi-day backpacks. There are trails on the floor of Yosemite Valley, trails that skirt its rim, and trails that explore the High Sierra above 8,000 feet. Lush meadows? Glacial lakes? Thirteen thousand-foot peaks? Check, check and check. The only question is where *not* to hike.

Yosemite's hiking season gears up in spring, when the Sierra Nevada's deep winter snowpack starts to melt. As the months progress, the snow line creeps higher and higher, and by mid-July most of the park's trails are usually open. But conditions vary considerably from year to year. Following particularly heavy winters, Yosemite's highest trails can stay buried until late July. Always check current conditions before hitting the trail. Yosemite National Park's official website (nps.gov/yose) lists current trail conditions, and the staff at Yosemite's Wilderness Centers are a terrific source of insider tips.

Hiking in spring and early summer can be great—waterfalls and wildflowers abound! But those months are also prime mosquito season. Fortunately, mosquito swarms are generally limited to the three weeks following snowmelt. But mosquitoes, like snowfall, vary considerably from year to year. Some years they're bad, some years they're not. Ask about mosquito conditions if you visit in May, June or July, and always pack repellent.

July and August are the most popular hiking months. Other than occasional afternoon thundershowers, days are gloriously sunny and dry. Nights, meanwhile, are cool and clear under an ocean of stars. September is one of the best months to hike thanks to reduced crowds and mild temperatures. By the end of September, however, temperatures at high elevations start to plunge. The first big snowfall usually hits around mid-November, at which point Tioga Road—the most popular gateway to the High Sierra—shuts down.

Day hikers can explore any trail, except Half Dome, without permits. Backpackers and Half Dome hikers must obtain permits, which are explained on the following page. Hikers should always carry a map and compass. My favorite topo map is National Geographic's *Trails Illustrated*, which shows day-use areas, campfire boundaries, and a wealth of other useful information.

Hiking Basics

- Carry and drink plenty of water
- Use good UV protection (high-SPF sunscreen, wide-brimmed hat)
- Pets and bicycles are only allowed on paved trails
- Horses and mules have the right of way
- Pack out what you pack in

Wilderness Permits

Wilderness permits are required for all overnight backpacks and Half Dome. Permits can be reserved in advance or picked up the day of, or the day before, the start of your hike at one of the park's five Wilderness Centers. Daily limits are placed on the number of permits issued for each trailhead. About 60% of permits for a given trailhead can be reserved up to 24 weeks in advance. The remaining 40% are available up to 24 hours in advance on a first-come, first-served basis. The reservation system, while sometimes frustrating, helps reduce overcrowding. By limiting the number of overnight hikers, the park ensures there are plenty of camping spots and a sense of solitude in the wilderness. Once you have a wilderness permit, it's great.

Permit reservation forms and trailhead availability are posted on the park's website (nps.gov/yose). When applying for a permit, you'll need the following information: entry trailhead, exit trailhead, dates of your trip, number of people in your party, and principal destination. Forms can be submitted online (yosemite.org), by phone (209-372-0740) or mail (Wilderness Permits, PO Box 545, Yosemite, CA 95389). Permits cost $5 per reservation, plus $5 per person. Try to pick up your permit the day before your hike. If you pick up a permit the day of your hike, arrive at the Wilderness Center as early as possible to avoid the long lines that form during peak season.

Wilderness Centers

Yosemite has five Wilderness Centers. They are located in Yosemite Valley, Tuolumne Meadows, Big Oak Flat Road, Wawona, and Hetch Hetchy. Badger Pass also operates a Wilderness Center in winter. Seasonal hours vary. Check the park's website or the *Yosemite Guide* for exact locations and hours of operation.

Backpacker Campgrounds

There are three Backpacker Campgrounds in Yosemite where backpackers with wilderness permits can spend the night before and after their trip without advance reservations. The park's Backpacker Campgrounds are located in Yosemite Valley, Tuolumne Meadows, and Hetch Hetchy.

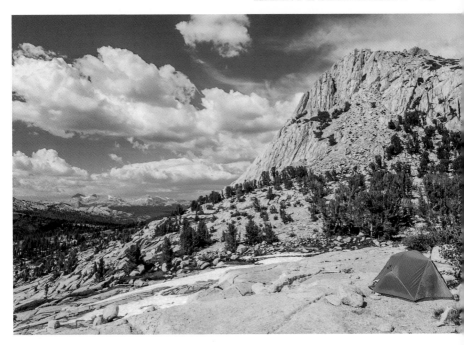

Weather Concerns

Sierra Nevada summers are generally sunny and dry. But anything can, and does, happen. The biggest concern is afternoon thundershowers, which build with alarming speed when monsoonal systems pass over the mountains from the east. Do not attempt any exposed hike (Half Dome, Clouds Rest, etc.) if you see dark clouds in the sky. If you see airplane contrails in the High Sierra before 10am, it means air moisture is higher than average, and a thunderstorm is likely between 2pm and 6pm. Always try to follow this rule: up high by noon, down low by two. And be aware that snow can fall at high elevations during any month of the year. Although summer snow is rare, it is possible, so be prepared. No matter when you hike, pack rain gear and warm clothes.

Guided Hikes & Backpacks

If you find Yosemite's vast network of trails intimidating, or you're new to hiking or backpacking, consider a guided hike. Some of the best guided hikes and backpacks are offered by the Yosemite Conservancy (yosemite.org, 209-379-2317), the nonprofit partner of Yosemite National Park. Their trips are led by local experts, many of whom specialize in natural history. Yosemite Conservancy also offers Half Dome hikes (they handle the permits!) and all-women backpacks. Aramark, Yosemite's concessionaire, also offers guided day hikes and overnight backpacks (travelyosemite.com, 209-372-8344).

Backpacking Rules

WATER

Purify all drinking water using a giardia-rated filter or iodine based chemical purifier, or by boiling 3–5 minutes.

CAMPFIRES

Campfires are prohibited above 9,600 feet. If you build a campfire below 9,600 feet, use only dead and fallen wood in a previously impacted fire ring.

CAMPSITES

Backcountry camping is prohibited within four miles of Yosemite Valley, Glacier Point, Tuolumne Meadows, Wawona and Hetch Hetchy. Backcountry camping is also prohibited within one mile of any road and within 100 feet of any water source. Campsites should be located at least 100 feet from the trail.

FOOD STORAGE

Overnight hikers must store their food in bear canisters (see below). Metal bear boxes are also provided at most trailheads.

SOAP & TOOTHPASTE

Never use soaps (even "biodegradable" ones) or toothpaste in any lake, river or stream. Use soap and toothpaste at least 100 feet away from any water source.

HUMAN WASTE

Backpackers must bury all human waste in a hole six inches deep at least 100 feet from any water source. Pack out all toilet paper.

Bear Canisters

Yosemite's black bears are generally harmless if undisturbed, but they are notorious for raiding backpackers' food. All wilderness backpackers must carry a bear canister to protect their food. In addition to keeping you safe, bear canisters prevent black bears from growing accustomed to human food.

Backpackers were once advised to place their food in a bag, tie the bag to a rope, and hang it from a tall branch at night. At first, this system worked. Then the bears got smart and started climbing out onto the branches. These days the bag-and-rope system has been abandoned in favor of rugged bear canisters that can hold up to a week's worth of food. You can purchase bear canisters at outdoor stores throughout California or rent them from any Yosemite Wilderness Center. Lock all food and scented items (toothpaste, soap, etc.) in your bear canister and place it at least 30 feet from your tent at night. Before going to bed, double check that all food has been removed from your tent.

Yosemite's Best Hikes

YOSEMITE VALLEY

The Mist Trail

GLACIER PT. ROAD

Pohono Trail

TIOGA ROAD

Clouds Rest

TUOLUMNE MEADOWS

ROCK CLIMBING

SAYING YOSEMITE IS a good place to climb rocks is like saying the Vatican is a good place to pray. To hardcore rock climbers, Yosemite is Mecca. Some of the world's most famous climbs are located in Yosemite Valley, and some of the sport's most innovative techniques and equipment were pioneered here. Yosemite's sheer granite walls attract tens of thousands of climbers each year. Beginners come to learn, intermediates spend years becoming experts, and experts follow in the footsteps (and footholds) of legends.

Rock climbing in Yosemite runs the gamut from easy bouldering (maneuvering across large boulders on the ground) to multi-day, 3,000-foot expeditions where climbers haul food, water and portable camping ledges. If a breezy night suspended thousands of feet above the ground doesn't inspire your inner Spider Man, there are other, less intimidating ways to enjoy the sport. The Yosemite Mountaineering School offers rock climbing lessons in Yosemite Valley from mid-April through October (travelyosemite.com, 209-372-8344). Yosemite Mountaineering School offers beginner, intermediate and advanced lessons, as well as two-day seminars on Big Wall Climbing. You can also hire private guides to lead you up Yosemite Valley's most storied climbs, including El Capitan and Half Dome. They supply the equipment, you supply the courage.

Summers are hot in Yosemite Valley (elevation: 4,000 feet), driving many rock climbers to the higher, cooler region around Tuolumne Meadows (elevation: 8,600 feet). In summer, Yosemite Mountaineering School operates a sister branch in Tuolumne Meadows (209-372-8435) that also offers climbing lessons.

A comprehensive guide to Yosemite rock climbing is far beyond the scope of this book. There are plenty of great climbing guidebooks available in stores throughout the park.

Despite rock climbing's inherent danger, there are relatively few climbing accidents in Yosemite. The key word is *relatively*. There are still, on average, over 100 climbing accidents each year. When bad weather or injuries threaten climbers' lives, Yosemite Search And Rescue (YOSAR) steps into action. This world-class climbing team scampers up and down vertical walls in harrowing conditions, performing complex rescue operations thousands of feet above the ground. Their exploits are legendary, and the rescue techniques they developed are used throughout the world.

For more on the history of rock climbing in Yosemite, see page 116.

Vogelsang

HIGH SIERRA CAMPS

YOSEMITE'S HIGH SIERRA Camps offer warm beds, hot showers, and hearty meals deep in the wilderness. There are five High Sierra Camps scattered throughout the park, each with a dining hall, restrooms, and canvas tent cabins heated by wood-burning stoves.

Every High Sierra Camp is located in a gorgeous setting, and the five camps are linked together in a 47-mile hiking loop. You can hike to any of the High Sierra Camps in a single day, or hike from camp to camp over several days. Nightly rates at High Sierra Camps (including meals) are $160/adult, $85/child.

Most visitors hike to the High Sierra Camps on their own, but multi-day guided hikes are also available. Five-day guided hikes cost $706/adult, $372/child. Seven-day guided hikes cost $1,048/adult, $553/child. Another option is a guided Saddle Trip, where you ride from camp to camp on a mule. Four-day guided Saddle Trips cost $1,292/adult, $1,040/child. Six-day guided Saddle Trips cost $2,014/adult, $1,601/child.

Yosemite's High Sierra Camps are normally open from early July to early September. But opening dates are sometimes pushed back following winters with heavy snow. Occasionally, following extremely snowy winters, the High Sierra Camps do not open at all.

Due to their popularity, High Sierra Camp reservations are granted by lottery in October. To enter the lottery visit travelyosemite.com or call 801-559-4884 for details and assistance. Lottery results are announced by email. If you missed the lottery, or didn't snag a golden ticket, High Sierra Camp cancellations sometimes become available on a first-come, first-served basis.

Note: most High Sierra Camp tent cabins are communal, which means you share the cabin with several other people. Communal cabins are often co-ed.

What's the best High Sierra Camp? It's all a matter of preference. There are no bad High Sierra Camps, but Vogelsang (located above treeline at 10,300 feet), Glen Aulin (situated next to a gorgeous waterfall along the Tuolumne River), and May Lake (located next to a stunning alpine lake in the heart of the park) never fail to please.

HIGH SIERRA CAMPS

Glen Aulin p.262

May Lake p.234

Cathedral Lakes

Tenaya Lake

Porcupine Flat

Olmstead Point

Sunrise p.240

North Dome

Half Dome

Glacier Point

Merced Lake

120

Young Lakes

Tioga Pass

Dog Lake

Tuolumne Meadows

Tioga Road

Tuolumne Lodge

Elizabeth Lake

Evelyn Lake

Ireland Lake

Vogelsang p.282

WINTER SPORTS

When PEOPLE THINK of Yosemite, they think of glorious summer days filled with hiking, rock climbing, and lots of Sierra sunshine. But the Sierra Nevada—the second-snowiest mountain range in North America, after the Cascades—is also a fantastic winter destination. There's plenty of winter fun in Yosemite, with a fraction of the summer crowds.

Badger Pass Ski Area (p.193), located 20 miles from Yosemite Valley off Glacier Point Road, is the oldest ski resort in California. The five-lift, ten-run mountain won't quicken the pulse of experts, but Badger Pass is a terrific beginner slope with reasonable prices. There's also snowtubing, snowshoeing, and over 100 miles of groomed and ungroomed cross-country trails. The cross-country highlight is skiing 10.5 miles from Badger Pass to Glacier Point (p.196), where you can spend the night in a cozy hut with warm meals (unguided: $143/night; guided: $452/one night, $562/two nights). The snowshoe highlight is a day trip to Dewey Point (p.206). Visit travelyosemite.com for details.

Another great option is an overnight cross-country ski trip to Ostrander Ski Hut ($50/night). The two-story stone hut, located at Ostrander Lake (p.204), has 25 beds, cooking facilities, and plenty of rustic charm (yosemite.org).

Tuolumne River

RIVER RAFTING

The MERCED RIVER, which twists and turns through Yosemite Valley, offers two kinds of rafting experiences: mellow and exciting.

Mellow: Curry Village rents four-person rafts to paddle down the Merced River in Yosemite Valley. You'll pass spectacular views of Half Dome, Yosemite Falls, and El Capitan as you float three gentle miles to Sentinel Beach, where a shuttle picks you up and takes you back to Curry Village. Raft rentals are available when the Merced isn't flowing too high or too low—a window that normally runs between late May and July. Cost: $30 per person.

Exciting: When the Merced River exits Yosemite, it roars through Class III & IV rapids alongside Highway 140. A handful of rafting companies offer half-day and full-day trips in the spring and early summer. Cost: around $150 per person. The best outfitters include OARS (800-346-6277, oars.com), Zephyr (800-431-3636, zrafting.com), ARTA (800-323-2782, arta.org), and Whitewater Voyages (800-400-7238, whitewatervoyages.com). OARS and Zephyr also offer day and overnight trips on the even wilder Tuolumne River, which boasts 18 miles of continuous Class IV rapids below Hetch Hetchy Reservoir. OARS even offers Tuolumne River trips that combine whitewater rafting during the day with gourmet food and wine/craft beer tastings at night!

Astronomy in Yosemite

With high elevations, clear skies, and minimal light pollution, Yosemite offers some of the best stargazing in California. If you're not looking up at night, you're missing half the show. Today nearly two-thirds of Americans live in cities and towns with so much light pollution they can no longer see the Milky Way. But here in Yosemite the Milky Way, which reveals the heart of our 200-billion-star galaxy, still blazes across the sky each night. Don't know much about astronomy? Inquire about Yosemite's free ranger astronomy programs. If you visit on a Saturday night in June, July, or August, swing by Glacier Point, where local astronomy clubs set up telescopes for public viewing. Aramark also offers Starry Night Skies Over Yosemite programs in both Yosemite Valley and at Glacier Point Visit travelyosemite.com for more info.

YOSEMITE BASICS

Getting to Yosemite

Yosemite's western entrances are located 60 miles northeast of Fresno (1.5-hour drive), 160 southeast of Sacramento (3.5-hour drive), 170 miles east of San Francisco (4-hour drive), and 280 miles northeast of Los Angeles (5-hour drive). Yosemite's only eastern entrance, Tioga Pass, is located 145 miles south of Reno, Nevada (3-hour drive). Visit jameskaiser.com for detailed driving routes, including sites and attractions along the way.

The closest international airports are located in Fresno and Reno. There's also a small regional airport at Mammoth Lakes, 33 miles from Tioga Pass. YARTS (Yosemite Area Regional Transportation System, 877-989-2787, yarts.com) offers seasonal and year-round buses to Yosemite Valley from nearby towns, including Fresno, Merced, Sonora, and Mammoth Lakes.

Yosemite Entrance Stations

Yosemite has three entrance stations along its western boundary (Big Oak Flat, Arch Rock, South Entrance) and one on its eastern boundary (Tioga Pass). Big Oak Flat Entrance, located along Highway 120, is the closest entrance to San Francisco. Arch Rock Entrance, located on Highway 140, is the closest entrance to the towns of Merced, Mariposa and Midpines. South Entrance, located along Highway 41 at the park's southern tip, offers quick access to Wawona and the Mariposa Grove of Giant Sequoias. Yosemite's only eastern entrance, Tioga Pass, is located at an elevation of 9,941 feet. Closed for much of the year due to snow, Tioga Pass is generally open late spring through mid-autumn and accessible from the small town of Lee Vining.

Entrance Fees

A seven-day pass to Yosemite National Park costs $35 per vehicle, $30 per motorcycle, or $20 per pedestrian or cyclist. An annual Yosemite pass costs $70. The best value, however, is the America the Beautiful Pass ($80), which gives you unlimited access to all U.S. national parks and federal recreation lands for one year. If you're 62 or older, the America the Beautiful Pass is good for life.

Getting Around Yosemite

The park operates free shuttles in Yosemite Valley throughout the year. In summer a shuttle runs along Tioga Road between Tioga Pass and Olmstead Point. Check the *Yosemite Guide* for seasonal schedules.

Information

As soon as you enter the park, pick up a copy of the *Yosemite Guide*. This free park publication, available at entrance stations and visitor centers, is filled with seasonal information, shuttle schedules, sunrise/sunset times, and other essential info. Ranger-staffed visitor centers are located in Yosemite Valley, Tuolumne Meadows and Wawona. There are also information booths in all park hotels. Yosemite's Twitter feed, @YosemiteNPS, is a great resource for up-to-the-minute weather updates and park alerts.

Gas

There are no gas stations in Yosemite Valley. The park's two gas stations, located at Crane Flat and Wawona, have 24-hour pumps. Although relatively pricey, both are cheaper than gas stations just outside the park.

One Perfect Day in Yosemite

The late, great Yosemite ranger Carl Sharsmith was once asked what he would do if he only had one day in Yosemite. His response: "I'd go down to the Merced River, put my head in my hands, and cry."

You could spend months exploring Yosemite, but it's possible to have a great time in the park in just one day. Head straight to Yosemite Valley (p.123) and bask in the park's most spectacular sights. Consider taking a narrated tram tour (p.125) in the morning, then pick up sandwiches at Degnan's (p.126). Head to the Mist Trail (p.168), hike to the top of Vernal Fall, and find a nice spot for a picnic lunch. Finish your day with a drive to Glacier Point (p.196) for sunset and stargazing. If Glacier Point feels a bit crowded, hike to the top of nearby Sentinel Dome (p.200).

Another Perfect Day in Yosemite

After exploring the highlights in Yosemite Valley, head to the High Sierra—the stunning alpine wilderness above 8,000 feet. Your adventure begins on Tioga Road (p.221), which passes impressive sights like the Tuolumne Grove of Giant Sequoias (p.224) and Olmstead Point (p.224). If you're short on time, drive as far as Tenaya Lake (p.229), where sparkling water reflects enormous granite domes. Otherwise, continue to Tuolumne Meadows (p.247), the largest high-altitude meadow in the Sierra Nevada. Hike to the top of Lembert Dome (p.256) for sweeping views of the surrounding scenery. For a dramatic drive with heart-stopping views, exit Yosemite through Tioga Pass (p.253), then descend the steep eastern flank of the Sierra Nevada.

When to Visit Yosemite

SPRING

Spring is the best season to visit Yosemite Valley. The waterfalls are at their peak, the wildflowers are blooming, and the summer crowds have not yet arrived. Daytime temperatures are often divine, but be prepared for chilly temperatures at night. In early spring, Tioga Road and Glacier Point Road are often closed due to lingering winter snow, restricting access to Tuolumne Meadows and Glacier Point. Both roads generally open by late May, but they can sometimes stay closed through June following winters with heavy snow.

SUMMER

Summer is Yosemite's busiest season. The park's famously sunny weather (just 3 percent of Yosemite's average annual precipitation falls in summer) draws a steady stream of vacationing families, which often means long lines and traffic jams in Yosemite Valley. By mid-summer many of Yosemite Valley's famous waterfalls have run dry, and daytime temperatures often soar into the 90s. For all of these reasons, savvy Yosemite visitors head to Tuolumne Meadows in July and August. While Yosemite Valley (4,000 feet) is hot and crowded, Tuolumne Meadows (8,600 feet) is a breath of fresh air.

FALL

Fall is a great time to visit Yosemite Valley. Crowds thin out after Labor Day, and daytime temperatures start to cool down. September is one of the best months for hiking and rock climbing in Yosemite Valley. In Tuolumne Meadows, September brings crisp days and freezing nights. Services shut down on Tioga Road by the end of September, and Tioga Road closes after the first heavy snow (generally sometime between mid-October and mid-November). In Yosemite Valley, even the biggest waterfalls slow to a trickle by mid-October, but this is also when colorful foliage lights up the park.

WINTER

Winter is the least popular season in terms of visitation, but after a fresh layer of snow Yosemite is spectacular. Tioga Road shuts down in winter, cutting off vehicle access to Tuolumne Meadows and the High Sierra. Glacier Point Road is plowed as far as Badger Pass, the oldest ski resort in California, which offers downhill and cross-country skiing, plus tubing and snowshoe walks. In Yosemite Valley, theAhwahnee Hotel offers wine tastings, Chefs' Holidays, and the famous Christmas Bracebridge Dinner. During the last two weeks of February, thousands of visitors arrive in Yosemite Valley to see the Firefall (p.157), Yosemite's most amazing natural spectacle. Note: all vehicles, including those with four-wheel-drive, must carry tire chains to enter the park in winter.

Black Bears

No other topic in Yosemite generates as much fear and confusion as black bears (p.76). Grainy videos of bears breaking into cars are played on a continuous loop on screens throughout the park, and overnight guests are required to sign forms stating they are "Bear Aware." Although black bears can sometimes be problematic, there's not much to worry about if you follow a few simple rules.

Yosemite's hungry black bears are not interested in eating you. But they're *very* interested in eating your food. Any food or scented items (toothpaste, sunscreen, etc.) left unattended or improperly stored attract bears, who have a powerful sense of smell. As a result, proper food storage is required at all times. Anything with a scent—canned goods, dirty dishes, even empty coolers—should be stored in metal food lockers, which are found throughout the park. Never leave any food or scented items in your tent or tent cabin. Never keep food in a hotel room with doors or windows left open. And never leave food in your car after daylight. Bears that see or smell food in cars will break windows and rip open doors. Bears sometimes break into cars after simply *seeing* a cooler. Failure to store your food properly can also result in a federal fine of up to $5,000!

If a bear approaches you in a developed area, make as much noise as possible to scare it away. This is easier said than done. But yelling or banging on pots and pans is often enough to scare bears away. Close bear encounters should also be reported to park rangers.

Backpackers must follow special food storage procedures (p.32) while camping in the wilderness. If you encounter a bear in the wilderness, maintain plenty of distance. This is especially important with cubs, because a highly protective mama bear might not be far behind.

Death In Yosemite

Most first-time Yosemite visitors worry about threats from bears and animals. But wildlife is among the least deadly of risks. No one has ever been killed by a bear in Yosemite, and only one person (a small child) died due to a rattlesnake bite. Horses, meanwhile, have been responsible for six deaths. Falling trees have killed nine people in the past 150 years, while rockfalls have killed 14.

Far more common is suicide. Over 60 people have taken their lives in the park. Over 100 people have died while rock climbing, and over 140 people have died from drowning. More than 40 people have been swept over waterfalls after swimming in the calm waters just above the falls.

So what's the biggest killer in Yosemite? Motor vehicles, which have killed over 160 people in the park.

Yosemite Lodging

Aramark (888-413-8869, travelyosemite.com) operates every lodge in Yosemite National Park. Be sure to make your reservations as far in advance as possible.

Lodging in Yosemite Valley

AHWAHNEE HOTEL

Yosemite's most luxurious lodge (p.162), with nearly 100 hotel rooms and 24 cottages. Rooms start at $375 per night and go higher than $1,000.

YOSEMITE VALLEY LODGE

Located steps from Yosemite Falls, Yosemite Valley Lodge offers 245 modern hotel rooms at reasonable rates. Facilities include two restaurants, a swimming pool, and a cozy bar filled with historic rock climbing photos. A few deluxe rooms have views of Yosemite Falls.

CURRY VILLAGE

The best budget lodging in Yosemite Valley. Over 400 canvas tent cabins with basic beds. Bathrooms and hot showers are available in communal bathhouses. Heated tent cabins are available in winter. There are also 46 wooden cabins with private baths, 14 cabins with a shared bathhouse, and 18 motel rooms.

HOUSEKEEPING CAMP

Home to 266 shelters consisting of three concrete walls, a canvas roof, and privacy curtains. Housekeeping Camp isn't luxurious, but its fabulous location on the sandy banks of the Merced River keeps visitors coming back year after year. All units include bunk beds and electrical outlets.

Other Lodging in the Park

TUOLUMNE MEADOWS LODGE

Tuolumne Lodge's 69 canvas tent cabins are similar to Curry Village tent cabins, but with wood-burning stoves to keep you warm at night. Bathrooms and hot showers are available in nearby communal bathhouses.

WHITE WOLF LODGE

Located just off Tioga Road, halfway between Yosemite Valley and Tuolumne Meadows, White Wolf Lodge has 24 canvas tent cabins with wood-burning stoves and four wooden cabins with propane heat. A rustic dining room serves meals.

WAWONA HOTEL

Located in Wawona, near the park's southern boundary, this historic hotel (established in 1856) is bursting with Victorian-era charm. Roughly half of the hotel's 104 rooms have private bathrooms, the rest offer shared bathrooms.

Yosemite Camping

Roughly half of Yosemite's 13 campgrounds are first-come, first-served. The rest require advance reservations (877-444-6777, recreation.gov). Most campsites can accommodate up to six people. Note: there is a 30-night camping limit in Yosemite National Park per calendar year. From May 1 to September 15, the camping limit in Yosemite is 14 nights, and only seven of those nights can be in Yosemite Valley or Wawona.

Camping in Yosemite Valley

Yosemite Valley (elevation 4,000 feet) is home to four campgrounds. The three "Pines" campgrounds are located at the eastern end of Yosemite Valley, and Camp 4 is located just east of Yosemite Falls. Book campsites as far in advance as possible (877-444-6777, recreation.gov). Hot showers can be purchased at Curry Village and Housekeeping Camp in the afternoon.

UPPER PINES CAMPGROUND

Open year-round, 238 sites, RVs up to 35 feet, $26/night.

LOWER PINES CAMPGROUND

Open April–October (approximately), 60 sites, RVs up to 40 feet, $26/night.

NORTH PINES CAMPGROUND

Open March–October (approximately), 81 sites, RVs up to 40 feet, $26/night.

CAMP 4

Popular with rock climbers, Camp 4 (p.136) is steeped in climbing history and jam-packed during peak climbing season. From late May through early September, campsites are available by daily lottery, one day in advance, at *recreation.gov*. The rest of the year Camp 4 is first-come, first-served. There are 36 walk-in sites for tents at a cost of $6 per person/night.

Camping in Tuolumne Meadows

There's only one campground in Tuolumne Meadows, but there are a handful of campgrounds between Yosemite Valley and Tuolumne Meadows along Tioga Road (see following page). There are also several small campgrounds located in Inyo National Forest just east of Tioga Pass (visit jameskaiser.com for more info).

TUOLUMNE MEADOWS CAMPGROUND

Yosemite's largest campground has 304 campsites. Half of the sites can be reserved, half are first-come, first-served. Open July to late September (weather permitting), RVs up to 35 feet, $26/night. Elevation: 8,600 feet. Hot showers can be purchased at nearby Tuolumne Lodge in the afternoon.

Other Campgrounds in the Park

BRIDALVEIL CREEK CAMPGROUND

Located roughly halfway up Glacier Point Road, Bridalveil Creek Campground is open July–September (weather permitting). First-come, first-served. 110 sites, $18/night, RVs up to 35 feet. Elevation: 7,200 feet.

CRANE FLAT CAMPGROUND

Located near the junction of Big Oak Flat Road and Tioga Road, Crane Flat Campground is open July to mid-October (weather permitting). Reservations available. 166 sites, $26/night, RVs up to 35 feet. Elevation: 6,200 feet.

HODGDON MEADOW CAMPGROUND

Located near Yosemite's Big Oak Flat Entrance, Hodgdon Meadow Campground is open year-round. Reservations required mid-April to mid-October. 105 sites, $26/night, RVs up to 35 feet. Elevation: 4,900 feet.

TAMARACK FLAT CAMPGROUND

Located off Tioga Road, not too far from Crane Flat, Tamarack Flat Campground is open late June–September (approximately). First-come, first-served. 52 sites, $12/night, no RVs. Elevation: 6,300 feet.

WHITE WOLF CAMPGROUND

Located next to White Wolf Lodge off Tioga Road, White Wolf Campground is open July to mid-September (weather permitting). First-come, first-served. 74 sites, $18/night, RVs up to 27 feet. Elevation: 8,000 feet.

YOSEMITE CREEK CAMPGROUND

Located off Tioga Road, Yosemite Creek Campground is open July–early September (approximately). First-come, first-served. 40 sites, $12/night, no RVs. Elevation: 7,700 feet.

PORCUPINE FLAT CAMPGROUND

Located along Tioga Road, Porcupine Flat Campground is open July–mid-October (approximately). First-come, first-served. 52 sites, $12/night, RVs up to 24 feet. Elevation: 8,100 feet.

WAWONA CAMPGROUND

Located in Wawona on the banks of the South Fork of the Merced River, Wawona Campground is open year-round. Reservations required mid-May to mid-October. 93 sites, $26/night, RVs up to 35 feet. Elevation: 4,000 feet.

For more Yosemite campground info, including photos and detailed descriptions, visit jameskaiser.com

Lodging & Camping Near Yosemite

There are dozens of hotels and campgrounds outside the park, and listing them all here would take dozens of pages. Rather than waste all that paper, I've posted comprehensive information about hotels and campgrounds just outside Yosemite online at jameskaiser.com.

Gateway Towns

MARIPOSA, MIDPINES & EL PORTAL

These three small towns, located west of Yosemite's Arch Rock Entrance along Highway 140, are the closest towns to Yosemite Valley. If you're planning on spending most of your time in Yosemite Valley, but every hotel in the park is booked, look for lodging in one of these towns. Mariposa (population: 2,000) located about 30 miles (45-minute drive) from Arch Rock Entrance Station, is a small Gold Rush-era town. Its boardwalk-lined Main Street is filled with boutiques, restaurants, and tap rooms. Mariposa is your best bet for dining outside the park, and there are several reasonably priced hotels. The tiny towns of Midpines (population: 1,200) and El Portal (population: 500) consist of a few scattered hotels and restaurants along Highway 140.

GROVELAND

Groveland (population: 600) is a Gold Rush-era town located along Highway 120 about 24 miles west of the park's Big Oak Flat Entrance. The town's most famous institution, the Iron Door Saloon, is the oldest continually operating saloon in California. It offers cold drinks, good food, and live entertainment on the weekends. Groveland also has a handful of charming B&Bs.

FISH CAMP & OAKHURST

Just outside the park's southern entrance is the tiny town of Fish Camp (population: 60), which is home to a small general store and a handful of B&Bs. Fourteen miles south of Fish Camp is Yosemite's largest gateway town, Oakhurst (population: 3,000). Downtown Oakhurst is filled with mini-malls and fast food restaurants. Like Mariposa, Oakhurst is a good bet for reasonably priced lodging if you don't mind the drive.

LEE VINING

The tiny town of Lee Vining (population: 200), located at the eastern base of the Sierra Nevada, revolves around Yosemite and Mono Lake tourism. If you're planning on spending the bulk of your time in Tuolumne Meadows but nearby lodges are booked, look for lodging in Lee Vining. Note: Tioga Road, which bisects the park and connects Lee Vining to Tuolumne Meadows and Yosemite Valley, is closed in winter due to snow.

GEOLOGY

YOSEMITE'S DAZZLING LANDSCAPE captivates every visitor who sets foot in the park. Stretching from the western foothills to the jagged crest of the Sierra Nevada Mountains, Yosemite encompasses some of America's most dramatic alpine scenery.

Even if you know nothing about geology, Yosemite is still an impressive sight. But take the time to learn about the forces that shaped it, and you'll look upon the park with a fresh set of eyes. What was once amazing will become astounding. What once took your breath away will make your head spin.

On a human timescale, Yosemite seems peaceful and serene. On a geological timescale, it's violent and exciting. The last glaciers to cover the park melted 10,000 years ago. In geological terms, 10,000 years is the blink of an eye. If Earth's age (4.5 billion years) was represented by a 24-hour clock, the past 10,000 years would represent just a fraction of the final second before midnight.

Yosemite's glaciers sculpted graceful valleys, gouged out sheer cliffs, and polished the granite to a shine. They also bulldozed soil and vegetation, scraping the surface clean and creating a frozen landscape nearly devoid of life. The most recent glacial advance started around 50,000 years ago, but at least three distinct periods of glacial advance—and possibly many more—have swept over the Sierra Nevada since the Ice Age began roughly 2.4 million years ago. Each glaciation added a new layer of depth and complexity to Yosemite's landscape, leaving behind thousands of dazzling new features. Few places in the world offer so many textbook-perfect examples of glacial geology.

Prior to the Ice Age, tectonic forces thrust up a massive, 400-mile long block of granite that created the Sierra Nevada. As the mountains rose, ancient rivers raced down their slopes, carving out deep valleys that, in places, exceed Grand Canyon in depth. By the time Ice Age glaciers arrived, the Sierra Nevada was already a fascinating landscape. Glaciers, it turns out, were simply the icing on an already remarkable cake.

ANCIENT ROCKS

YOSEMITE'S STORY BEGAN roughly 500 million years ago when North America was situated near the equator and California lay under a warm tropical sea. As rivers flowed into the sea, they flushed massive amounts of sediment offshore. Over millions of years, sediment layers grew thousands of feet thick, and the bottom-most layers were compressed into sedimentary rocks. Then, as tectonic plates shifted, North America rotated and moved north. During this time tectonic forces also pushed up the underwater sedimentary rocks, forming the ancient surface of California.

Around 200 million years ago, North America collided with a vast tectonic plate called the Farallon Plate, which lay under the ocean to the west. As the North American Plate overrode the Farallon Plate—a process geologists call *subduction*—the Farallon Plate dove several miles beneath North America, and extreme heat and pressure melted its leading edge. Vast pools of magma rose up under California, some of which reached the surface to form volcanoes. Most of the magma, however, cooled deep underground into granite.

For the next 130 million years, as subduction of the Farallon Plate continued, enormous quantities of magma rose under California in giant plumes called plutons. The plutons arrived in a series of pulses that lasted between ten million and 15 million years. By about 80 million years ago, the combined plutons formed a giant, underground mass of granite called a batholith (from the Greek words *bathos*, "deep," and *lithos*, "rock"). Throughout the formation of the Sierra Nevada Batholith, intense temperatures and pressures cooked the overlying sedimentary rocks, altering their chemical composition. Over time these sedimentary rocks were transformed (metamorphosed) into metamorphic rocks.

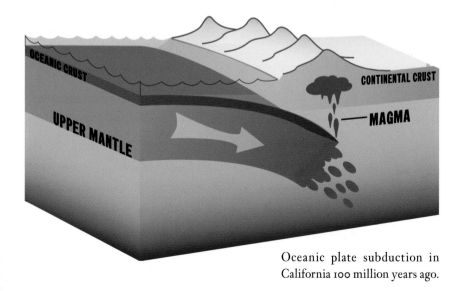

Oceanic plate subduction in California 100 million years ago.

THE MOUNTAINS RISE

AS SUBDUCTION SENT massive pools of magma rising under California, a chain of active volcanoes formed on the surface that, at their peak, may have towered as high as 18,000 feet. Then, around 80 million years ago, the magma stopped rising. The volcanoes became inactive, and for the next 40 million years erosion ground down the mountains, removing the overlying metamorphic rock and exposing the underlying granite.

When the mountains rose up, the gradients of mountain rivers increased, speeding their flow and accelerating erosion. The rivers carved deep canyons and flushed millions of tons of sediment into California's Central Valley, which lies just west of the Sierra Nevada. (Drive across the Central Valley today and you are driving across eroded Sierra Nevada sediments that sometimes reach depths of tens of thousands of feet.)

Around 20 million years ago, the western edge of North America came into contact with a new tectonic plate, the Pacific Plate, which underlies much of the Pacific Ocean. But the collision between the Pacific Plate and the North American Plate was not head-on. Rather, the plates moved laterally in opposite directions, grinding against each other along their boundary. This boundary, which still exists today, is called the San Andreas Fault.

As the two tectonic plates scraped against each other along the San Andreas Fault, huge pressures built up among interlocking rocks. Ultimately the rocks buckled and broke—a sudden pressure release that caused (and continues to cause) earthquakes. But not all of the built-up pressure concentrated on the San Andreas Fault. The force of the grinding plates fanned out across California, cracking the land and forming new, smaller faults.

As complex pressures exerted themselves from multiple directions, a fault system formed near the eastern edge of the Sierra Nevada Batholith. The land rose up as if on a pivot from the west, creating a sheer eastern slope and a long, gentle western slope. Uplift started slowly around ten million years ago, then accelerated several million years later. Eventually, the modern Sierra Nevada Mountains towered 14,000 feet above the landscape.

Throughout the uplift of the Sierra Nevada, millions of cracks formed in the underlying granite. Some cracks formed due to pressures associated with uplift. Other cracks formed as erosion stripped away miles of overlying rocks, causing the underlying rocks to expand and crack. These cracks (called joints) still form today. Extending in every direction, they create a giant template for future erosion. Some cracks are vertical, some are horizontal, and some form in rounded concentric layers. The concentric cracks are the most fascinating because they flake off like layers of an onion, leaving behind dramatic rounded domes in a process called *exfoliation*.

ICE AGE GLACIERS

AROUND 2.4 MILLION years ago, Earth entered the Ice Age. As global temperatures cooled and snowfall increased, a thick snowpack accumulated in the Sierra Nevada that, over time, compacted into massive ice sheets. Eventually the ice sheets began moving under the pressure of their own weight, at which point they became glaciers. Pushing downhill, the glaciers consumed everything in their path. Boulders, soil, trees—everything but the bedrock was picked up and carried along. But even the bedrock did not escape unscathed. The glaciers, which were full of debris, acted like giant sheets of sandpaper, grinding down the bedrock and smoothing it out.

Then, abruptly, temperatures warmed and the glaciers retreated. Then they advanced and retreated again. And again. Over the past 2.4 million years, as global temperatures fluctuated, glaciers advanced and retreated at least three times in the Sierra Nevada. At even higher latitudes glaciers advanced and retreated over a dozen times, and many geologists believe that Sierra Nevada glaciers followed a similar pattern. But because Sierra Nevada glaciers erased everything in their path, including evidence of previous glaciations, supporting facts are scarce.

The oldest and largest glacial advance in the Sierra Nevada, known as the pre-Tahoe glaciation, occurred roughly 1 million years ago. As pre-Tahoe glaciers descended from high elevations, they blanketed the mountains under a massive sheet of ice roughly 270 miles long by 40 miles wide. Only the highest peaks in the Sierra Nevada remained exposed, poking out like rocky islands in a sea of ice. All told, over half of Yosemite was covered by ice. Tuolumne Meadows was buried under 2,000 feet of ice, and Yosemite Valley was filled to the brim.

The force of the glaciers was massive. Under the largest glaciers, pressures topped several hundred pounds per square inch. Where the bedrock was weakened by cracks, glaciers plucked out large chunks of rock and carried them to lower elevations. Where bedrock was solid and relatively free of cracks, glaciers smoothed out the rock and formed *glacial polish*—a glassy veneer with a texture as smooth as polished marble. Sometimes the glacial polish was later scraped by rocks embedded at the bottom of the glacier, leaving behind distinct scratches called *glacial striations*.

Descending from high elevations, at speeds ranging from several inches to several feet per day, glaciers flowed through previously formed river valleys that, cut by pre-Ice Age rivers, had steep V-shaped profiles. As the glaciers advanced through the V-shaped valleys, they gouged out the sides and left rounded U-shaped valleys in their wake.

Meanwhile, the front of the glaciers acted like giant bulldozers pushing accumulated debris. When the glaciers reached lower, warmer elevations, their leading edges melted, depositing the accumulated debris. Ice continued to flow from

above, however, forming a kind of conveyor belt that transported even more loose material to the melting front of the glacier. The debris piles that formed are called terminal moraines, and they mark the farthest extent of the glaciers. A similar feature, called lateral moraines, formed along the sides of glaciers. Today many remnant terminal and lateral moraines clearly mark the maximum extent of their glaciers.

During each of the Sierra Nevada glaciations, the glaciers advanced for tens of thousands of years. But as global temperatures warmed, the glaciers melted, and large boulders embedded in the ice settled on top of the underlying bedrock. These rocks, which were often carried miles from their points of origin, are called glacial erratics, and they remain scattered throughout the High Sierra today.

At the end of the most recent glaciation—the Tioga glaciation, which ended roughly 10,000 years ago—temperatures warmed and glaciers started to melt. By about 8,000 years ago, glaciers had completely disappeared from the Sierra Nevada. Since then, however, fluctuations in climate have triggered at least two additional periods of glacial advance and retreat, though on a much smaller scale. The most recent glaciation occurred from 1600 to 1850, when temperatures dropped during a period of global cooling called the Little Ice Age. During this time, roughly 100 small glaciers formed in the Sierra Nevada. But over the past 150 years, as global temperatures rose, many of those glaciers melted. Today in Yosemite only a handful of small glaciers remain.

Glacial Landscapes

As massive glaciers advanced over the High Sierra during the last Ice Age, they rounded and smoothed the underlying granite. Today graceful, glacially sculpted landscapes are visible throughout Yosemite's high elevations.

Nunataks

At the height of the Ice Age one million years ago, only Yosemite's tallest peaks remained above the glaciers, poking out like rocky islands in a sea of ice. Although the glaciers rounded and smoothed the lower mountain slopes, their summits remained jagged and rough. Today these angular peaks, called nunataks, can be seen throughout the High Sierra.

GEOLOGY TODAY

GLACIERS PUT THE finishing touches on the Sierra Nevada, but erosion continues to chip away at the mountains. One of the most common forms of erosion is frost wedging, which occurs when water freezes and expands in the cracks of rocks, eventually breaking them apart. Frost wedging is most active in spring and fall when daily temperature fluctuations are greatest.

Earthquakes are also common in the Sierra Nevada, which is riddled with active faults along its eastern boundary. In 1872 an earthquake struck near Lone Pine, California, which lies at the base of the eastern Sierra. The earthquake, which was probably more powerful than the 1906 San Francisco earthquake, killed 27 people and pulverized nearly every building in town. In an instant, the mountains above Lone Pine jumped 13 feet higher and shifted 20 feet laterally. In Yosemite Valley, the early morning earthquake woke up John Muir, who stumbled outside to watch a rocky pinnacle crash to the ground. An observer near Nevada Falls claimed the waterfall stopped flowing for at least half a minute. At nearby Liberty Cap, thousands of tons of rock shook free, creating a powerful air blast that knocked a building off its foundation.

Rockfalls are one of the most significant forms of erosion acting on Yosemite today. They can be triggered by earthquakes, frost wedging, or other forms of erosion. Sometime around 1740, a massive rockfall took out 5.6 million tons of Slide Mountain (later named for the rock slide) in a remote, northern section of the park. Dozens of smaller rockfalls have taken place since, including a 2006 rockfall along the Merced River Canyon west of Yosemite Valley. That rockfall buried 600 feet of Highway 140 and closed the road for nearly two months. As the years progress, erosion will slowly chip away at these rockfalls, reducing boulders to talus, talus to scree, scree to gravel, and gravel to sand.

Parts of the eastern Sierra Nevada are also volcanically active. Mammoth Mountain, home to a popular ski resort southeast of Yosemite, is a volcano that formed 400,000 years ago. A large magma chamber also exists under Mono Basin directly east of Yosemite. The last known volcanic event in the region was a mild underwater eruption at the bottom of Mono Lake in 1890. When, or where, the next eruption will occur is unknown.

Moving forward, the forces of geology will continue to reshape the landscape in subtle and not-so-subtle ways. Over hundreds of years, rockfalls will continue to erode Yosemite's cliffs. Over tens of thousands of years, if humans successfully reduce greenhouse gas emissions, vast glaciers could theoretically cover the mountains again. And over millions of years, the park's most stunning features—Half Dome, El Capitan, Yosemite Falls—will disappear entirely. So consider yourself lucky. You're alive for that brief moment, geologically speaking, when Yosemite is filled with world-class scenery.

Muir v. Whitney

The Formation of Yosemite Valley

JOHN MUIR

When members of California's State Geologic Survey first studied Yosemite Valley in the 1860s, they found themselves perplexed. Unlike most glacially sculpted valleys, which have a graceful U-shape, Yosemite Valley has sheer vertical cliffs rising from a flat floor. Given this unusual topography, the Survey determined that Yosemite Valley was not, in fact, sculpted by glaciers. Instead, they theorized that it was created by a sudden, cataclysmic event—perhaps a massive earthquake that caused the floor of Yosemite Valley to drop down.

Scruffy nature writer John Muir (p.102) vehemently disagreed with the Survey's cataclysmic "drop down" theory. Having carefully studied the effects of glaciers during his extensive wanderings in the High Sierra, Muir was convinced that Yosemite Valley had been sculpted by glaciers. Although Muir studied geology during his last two years at the University of Wisconsin, he was a scientific amateur, and members of the Geologic Survey laughed off his theory as nonsense. Josiah Whitney, the Yale-educated head of the Survey, insisted there was no evidence to indicate glaciers had ever occupied Yosemite Valley.

Muir held his ground, and the more he lectured on his glacial formation theory, the more people listened. Finally, in 1870, Muir's theory was officially endorsed by the famous Harvard geologist Louis Agassiz and his student Dr. Joseph Le Conte, a professor at the University of California. Members of the Geologic Survey were appalled. They hurled insults at Muir, calling him an "ignoramus" and "a mere sheepherder." Whitney stated that the glacier theory was "based on entire ignorance of the whole subject, [and] may be dropped without wasting any more time upon it."

In fact, the debate raged on for nearly 60 years. Then, in 1930, long after the deaths of both Whitney and Muir, the distinguished French geologist François Matthes announced that he agreed with Muir's theory, and the matter was finally laid to rest. In hindsight, Muir's theory, although extremely close, was not entirely correct. And while Whitney was wrong about the formation of Yosemite Valley, he did correctly identify Hetch Hetchy as a glacially sculpted valley. Today John Muir's likeness is portrayed on the California quarter, while the highest mountain in California is named after Josiah Whitney.

JOSIAH WHITNEY

Rockfalls in Yosemite

Ever since Ice Age glaciers melted 10,000 years ago, rockfalls have been the main geologic force sculpting Yosemite. On average, there is a rockfall every ten days in Yosemite Valley. And while the vast majority are small and insignificant, large rockfalls occasionally prove catastrophic.

One of the most famous rockfalls occurred in 1996 at the eastern end of Yosemite Valley. High above Happy Isles, two rocks totaling 40,000 cubic yards in size detached from the cliffs above. The rocks hit the ground traveling at 270 miles per hour, and the resulting wind blast exceeded 250 miles per hour. Over 900 trees toppled like matchsticks, and one hiker was killed. (All told, 15 people have died due to rockfalls in Yosemite). The largest historic rockfall in Yosemite Valley occurred in 1987, when roughly 800,000 cubic yards of debris tumbled down from the Three Brothers, closing Northside Drive for months.

But even these rockfalls pale in comparison to the mega-rockfalls known as rock avalanches. No rock avalanches have occurred in Yosemite Valley in recorded history, but evidence of their past destruction abounds. Roughly 3,600 years ago, 3.75 million cubic yards of rock fell 2,500 feet down the eastern face of El Capitan. The resulting debris pile spread 2,200 feet past the base of El Capitan. An even larger rock avalanche occurred in Tenaya Canyon, when *10 million* cubic yards of rock tumbled down the cliffs across from Half Dome. The resulting debris pile, 100 feet deep in places, dammed Tenaya Creek and created Mirror Lake.

Interestingly, relatively few rockfalls occur on Yosemite Valley's lower cliffs. That's because Ice Age glaciers, which never reached the rim during the last glaciation, scraped away loose rocks from the lower cliffs. As a result, most Yosemite Valley rockfalls occur on the upper cliffs, which gives them even more destructive energy when they crash down.

Although relatively common, rockfalls remain shrouded in mystery. Geologists know they can be triggered by earthquakes, the expansion of freezing water in cracks, and other erosive processes. But the exact trigger of many rockfalls is hard to determine. In a park as popular as Yosemite, the ability to understand and predict rockfalls could save many lives. But rockfall prediction, like earthquake prediction, has proven quite challenging.

Although rockfalls have historically been difficult to study, new technologies are starting to reveal their secrets. Geologists now use high-resolution photography and LIDAR (terrain mapping with lasers) to make high-resolution 3D maps of Yosemite's cliffs. By cross-referencing data from year to year, computers can determine where small sections of cliffs are missing, revealing previously unreported rockfalls. And thanks to smartphones, more and more rockfalls are

Slide Mountain

GREAT BASIN DESERT

SIERRA NEVADA

Lake
Tahoe

Yosemite
National
Park

Mono
Lake

SIERRA NEVADA

GREAT CENTRAL VALLEY

Pacific Ocean

Sierra Nevada Mountains

Running half the length of California, the Sierra Nevada is the longest, highest mountain range in America. Although the Rocky Mountains and Appalachian Mountains are longer, they are technically mountain *systems* made up of several smaller ranges. The Sierra Nevada, by contrast, is a single unbroken range that's nearly as large as the French, Swiss, and Italian Alps combined. At roughly 26,000 square miles, the Sierra Nevada covers nearly 20 percent of California.

From Fredonyer Pass in the north to Tehachapi Pass in the south, the Sierra Nevada stretches 420 miles, varying in width from 50 to 80 miles. The mountains are essentially a massive block of granite lifted like a trap-door on a western hinge. The long western slope rises gradually at a tilt of just 2 to 6 degrees, while the steep eastern slope plummets 25 degrees, dropping over two vertical miles in places.

Sierra Nevada peaks increase in elevation from north to south, reaching 10,000 feet near Lake Tahoe, 13,000 feet in Yosemite, and 14,000 feet near Mt. Whitney. At 14,495 feet, Mt. Whitney is the tallest peak in the lower 48 states. All told, the entire range contains roughly 500 peaks above 12,000 feet. Over half of the alpine Sierra Nevada (the area located above treeline) is exposed rock, and nearly all of it is protected as national parks or federally designated wilderness.

The Sierra Nevada is bounded on the west by California's Great Central Valley, where flat agricultural lands grow one quarter of America's food. As coastal air flows over the Sierra Nevada from the west, it rises and cools, wringing out nearly all of its moisture. Dry air then flows down the Sierra Nevada's eastern slope, creating the Great Basin Desert.

Sierra Nevada summers are generally dry, but winters can dump up to 70 feet of snow. The heaviest snowfall occurs in the Central Sierra, which bears the brunt of winter storms that pass through San Francisco's Golden Gate—the most prominent gap in California's coastal mountains. In spring, a combination of rain and snowmelt brings heavy runoff to the mountains. By autumn, however, many streams have slowed to a trickle.

Only a handful of rivers tumble down the Sierra's steep eastern flank. Flowing into the Great Basin Desert, their waters never reach the sea. On the gentle western slope, 11 major rivers flow into the Central Valley, eight of which join the Sacramento and San Joaquin rivers on their journey to the San Francisco Bay. Many western Sierra Nevada rivers have cut dramatic valleys thousands of feet deep. The largest, Kings Canyon, is deeper than Grand Canyon, with walls over 7,000 feet high.

Lyell Glacier

Resting on the northern slope of Mt. Lyell (the highest peak in the park), Lyell Glacier was once the largest glacier in Yosemite, the second largest glacier in the Sierra Nevada, and one of the southernmost glaciers in North America. Both the mountain and the glacier were named for Charles Lyell, whose 1830 book *Principles of Geology* has been called "the most seminal work in geology." (Ironically, when the theory of ice ages was first advanced in the 1830s, Lyell did not believe it, and he argued against it for decades.) Over the past century, however, Lyell Glacier shrunk significantly due to warming temperatures. In 2013 it was determined that Lyell Glacier was no longer moving, and thus should be technically classified as an "ice field."

Lyell Glacier, 2006

ECOLOGY

COVERING OVER 1,000 square miles and featuring over 10,000 feet of elevation change, Yosemite shelters a fascinating ecosystem home to thousands of plants and animals. Giant sequoias, the largest organisms on the planet, have lived at the park's lower elevations for thousands of years. Delicate alpine flowers, meanwhile, measure their lives in weeks among the park's highest peaks. The forests between are home to black bears, mountain lions, mule deer, and dozens of smaller animals. All told, over 80 mammal species, over 260 bird species, and over 1,400 plant species have been identified in the park.

Plants and animals live only where factors such as temperature, sunlight, nutrients and water favor their survival. Plants form the foundation of a thriving food chain, and ecologists have divided the Sierra Nevada into half a dozen vegetative zones—five of which occur in Yosemite. These zones, based loosely on elevation, provide an easy way to visualize a complex system. But boundaries between zones are often fuzzy, with some species living in two or three zones, and microclimates further blur the distinctions. This complexity is a reflection of the dramatic landscape. Driving from the arid plains of the Central Valley to Tioga Pass—at 9,943 feet the highest paved road in California—is the ecological equivalent of driving from Mexico to Alaska in a single day.

The Sierra Nevada Mountain Range boasts many impressive statistics. It's the highest unbroken mountain range in the continental U.S. and the second snowiest mountain range in North America (after the Cascade Range in the Pacific Northwest). Over 3,500 plant species live in the Sierra Nevada—a number greater than the total number of plant species found in Florida. And the Sierra Nevada's alpine region, which lies above treeline, has the richest flora of any alpine area in North America. Nearly 200 plant species that grow in the Sierra Nevada are found nowhere else in the world.

Like environments everywhere, the Sierra Nevada are constantly changing. Geological forces, fluctuating climate, and human influences that began thousands of years ago have all shaped the present environment. And they will continue to shape it in the years to come. How Yosemite's ecology took shape, and how it continues to evolve, is one of the park's most fascinating stories.

A CHANGING LANDSCAPE

YOSEMITE'S MODERN ECOLOGY started to take shape around 15,000 years ago when Ice Age glaciers began to melt. Those glaciers, which covered much of the Sierra Nevada, scraped away soil and vegetation, and when the ice melted it revealed a vast, barren landscape. Hundreds of square miles of sparkling granite billowed down from the highest peaks. Bedrock depressions scooped out by the glaciers filled with meltwater, creating thousands of new ponds and lakes. But at that time much of the landscape was essentially lifeless.

The formation of soil, a combination of eroded rock and decomposed organic material, was a very slow process. Granite is one of the world's most erosion-resistant rocks, and the glaciers left little organic material in their wake. But over thousands of years, as lichens and other hardy colonizers gained a foothold, a thin layer of topsoil built up, making the mountains habitable for progressively larger plants. Eventually, enough topsoil formed to support sun-loving trees, which thrived in the open, sunny landscape. After a shady forest canopy developed, shade-loving trees also took root.

Ecologists call this ongoing process of new plant arrival in response to changing conditions *succession*. In the long term, succession occurs as the fluctuating climate alters temperature and precipitation, which changes the composition of forests and meadows. In the short term, succession occurs when forests are disturbed by fire, avalanches, or insect infestations. As the composition of the forest changes, so do the plant and animal species living there. Some species thrive in sunny open spaces, while others prefer shady mature forests.

Over the past 10,000 years, as environmental conditions changed, the Sierra Nevada's ecology changed with them. Temperatures warmed considerably after the Ice Age, but the rate of warming has not been steady. As temperatures fluctuated, Sierra Nevada vegetation marched up and down the mountains, shifting to higher elevations during warm periods and retreating to lower elevations during cool periods. The changing climate also affected precipitation. The past 1,200 years have seen two major droughts, each lasting 100 to 200 years, while the past 150 years have been relatively warm and wet, including one of the wettest half centuries of the past 1,000 years. All of these factors, combined with modern human influences, have affected forest density and wildfire patterns, laying the groundwork for present conditions.

The Sierra Nevada Mountains cover just 20 percent of California, but they contain over half of the state's 7,000 plant species. Roughly one-third of Sierra Nevada plant species are found nowhere else in the world.

ECOLOGY TODAY

OVER 95 PERCENT of the Sierra Nevada's annual precipitation falls between October and April, and winters bring massive amounts of snow—up to 50 feet in some places. Summers, by contrast, are hot and dry, resulting in less than 5 percent of the region's annual precipitation. No other mountain range in North America has seasonal weather as varied and dramatic as that of the Sierra Nevada. And this has profound implications for the plants and animals living there.

After surviving summer droughts and deep winter snows, plants and animals must contend with massive spring runoff. Three-quarters of Sierra Nevada snowpack melts between April and June. The combined outflow of rivers and streams can be ten times larger than the flow of the Colorado River, which drains seven western states. But precipitation is highly variable, and runoff in wet years can be up to *20 times* greater than runoff in dry years.

Thousands of streams tumble down the Sierra Nevada, coalescing into 11 major rivers on the western slope. Yosemite is home to two of those major rivers: the Merced and the Tuolumne, which drain 511 square miles and 680 square miles respectively in the park. All told, over 1,600 miles of streams flow through Yosemite.

Many of Yosemite's streams are fed by high-elevation lakes, which generally support few plants or animals due to lack of nutrients. Alpine lakes are considered biologically poor because the surrounding vegetation is sparse and organic debris is limited. Some alpine lakes have a striking turquoise color due to *glacial flour*—extremely fine rock particles, ground down by glaciers, that are flushed into high-elevation lakes. Suspended in the otherwise clear water, glacial flour reflects blue and green light wavelengths.

At lower elevations with more vegetation, lakes are more nutrient-rich, and thus support a thriving food chain. Over time, however, as organic debris accumulates and tributary streams deposit additional sediments, the lakes eventually fill in. Many low-elevation meadows are former lakes that filled with sediment and organic debris. Many of those meadows, in turn, will eventually be invaded by saplings and trees. This successional process has turned many former lakes into meadows and forests, including a massive prehistoric lake that once filled Yosemite Valley.

Not all meadows turn into forests. Some meadows exist due to naturally soggy soil, which prevents the growth of trees. Although Yosemite's meadows constitute just three percent of the park's total area, they are frequently hotspots of biodiversity. Up to one-third of Yosemite plant species grow in meadows, including the Yosemite bog orchid, which was discovered in 2003. Meadows also provide valuable habitats for mammals such as mule deer, Belding's ground squirrels, and pocket gophers.

Sierra Nevada soil fertility is generally poor due to the short, dry growing season. But the mountains are perfect for conifers. Most of the bedrock is granite, which breaks down into thin, coarse-grained soil that favors conifers such as lodgepole pines and ponderosa pines. Nearly half of all Sierra Nevada trees are conifers. By comparison, conifers represent just 10 percent of trees in the Southeastern United States.

Roughly 90 percent of the Sierra Nevada is covered in vegetation. Forests dominate Yosemite's scenery from the park's lowest elevations to treeline, which occurs at roughly 10,400 feet. Treeline is determined by a number of factors, including soil, precipitation, wind and the length of the growing season. But the limiting factor is cold. If an area is too cold, no tree will survive, no matter how favorable the other conditions.

Interestingly, it's not winter cold but summer cold that determines treeline. Although Sierra Nevada trees can survive below average winter temperatures, they cannot withstand those temperatures year-round. Summer temperatures must average 50° F or greater for a tree to grow. If a certain location experiences average temperatures below 50° F in July, no trees will grow there.

Treeline is a loose boundary, however, with short scraggly trees finding a way to scrape out a living above 10,400 feet. Some trees grow at dwarf sizes. Others put down roots in warm microclimates that allow them to grow at slightly higher elevations. The absolute limit of treeline, above which no tree can grow, is called the krummholz limit (*Krummholz* is the German word for "twisted tree"). In Yosemite, whitebark pine dominates treeline, along with shrubs such as willows, buckwheats and currants.

Above treeline lies the alpine zone—a harsh, beautiful landscape filled with sparkling granite. The Sierra Nevada alpine zone stretches over 150 unbroken miles from Mt. Whitney to Sonora Pass, just north of Yosemite. Many hikers and backpackers consider this region to be the most spectacular part of Yosemite, but heavy snow covers the landscape for much of the year, making it accessible only in summer and fall.

Due to the alpine zone's short growing season, alpine plants flower and fruit much faster than plants growing at lower elevations. As a result, their reproductive cycle is condensed into weeks instead of months. Plants are extremely active in summer, photosynthesizing rapidly during the long, sunny days before cold temperatures and limited sunlight return.

Animals in the alpine zone have also adapted to the inhospitable landscape. Many alpine mammals have thick fur and rounded bodies, which maximize volume and minimize heat loss. When winter arrives, most alpine zone animals descend to lower, warmer elevations in search of food. Only a few rugged animals remain in this frigid region year-round.

HUMAN IMPACT

WHEN EUROPEANS FIRST visited the Sierra Nevada Mountains, they marveled at the sunny, open forests. Trees were spaced widely apart, and the forest floor was relatively free of debris. According to one early report, you could ride a horse at full gallop through the forest. Unknown to the new arrivals, these beautiful, open landscapes were the result of frequent fires.

Small fires caused by lightning strikes historically swept through Sierra Nevada forests about once every decade. Regular fires played an important role in the ecosystem, clearing out brush and debris, returning nutrients to the soil, killing insect pests, and destroying saplings that competed with older trees. Large trees, protected by thick bark, not only survived small fires, they thrived in the fire's nutrient-rich wake. In a typical year, thousands of acres might burn in the Sierra Nevada. Some estimates indicate that, historically, over two percent of Yosemite burned each year.

Native tribes also set intentional fires to maintain open forests and meadows. This reduced the buildup of underbrush and saplings, which otherwise fueled large wildfires that could destroy mature trees. Acorns were an important food source for native tribes, so protecting mature oak trees from large wildfires was critical. Intentional fires also created prime habitat for wild game like deer, and the open spaces made hunting much easier. For native tribes, fire was a powerful landscape management tool.

After the arrival of Europeans, disease and genocide decimated native populations, and manmade fires became increasingly rare. In the mid-1800s, however, sheepherders began setting intentional fires in the Sierra Nevada to keep meadows open and increase the number of edible grasses for grazing animals. According to one sheepherder, "We started setting fires and continued setting them until we reached the foothills. We burned everything that would burn."

By the late 1890s, when Yosemite National Park and Sequoia National Park were established, the federal government had established a policy of fire suppression to protect and preserve the landscape. The way they saw it, fire marred the scenery, threatened wildlife, and contaminated watersheds. Although the wisdom of fire suppression was questioned by some, it became the dominant forest management policy for the next half century.

Government-sponsored fire suppression, combined with the disappearance of intentionally set human fires, radically transformed forests in the Sierra Nevada. In some places, natural burning was reduced by 98 percent, and many previously open forests became choked with thick underbrush and young saplings. Eventually a shady canopy developed that encouraged shade-loving trees such as white fir and incense cedar to invade the landscape. Saplings also invaded mountain meadows, which had historically been kept open by fire. By the 1940s, much of the Sierra Nevada was overgrown and, in many ways, unnatural.

CALIFORNIA GRIZZLIES

CALIFORNIA REPUBLIC

Prior to European contact, grizzly bears were abundant throughout California. The range of these highly adaptable animals covered most of the state, excluding the eastern deserts and the High Sierra. "It was not uncommon to see thirty to forty a day," noted an observer in the Sacramento Valley in 1841. By 1922, however, not a single grizzly bear remained in California. The state's entire grizzly population, once estimated at nearly 10,000 bears, had been killed by hunters.

Grizzlies are the largest and most powerful bears in North America. Weighing up to 1,500 pounds, they are omnivores that require vast quantities of food, eating plants, animals, insects, and just about anything else. When Spanish settlers arrived in California in the 1600s, some grizzlies found it easier to kill cattle and livestock than to hunt wild food. Before long, Mexican ranchers were capturing live grizzlies for bull-and-bear fights, where the two animals, tethered together, fought to the death. Grizzlies generally won the first round, at which point ranchers tied up a new bull. Such spectacles supposedly influenced New York newspaper editor Horace Greeley to coin the terms "bull market" and "bear market," because the bull—or more accurately *bulls*—always won.

During the Bear Flag Revolt of 1846, American settlers revolted against Mexican authorities in California. After a swift victory, the Americans raised a new flag that featured a grizzly bear. The flag had a brief career, however, flying less than a month before it was replaced by the Stars and Stripes. In 1911 a modified version of the Bear Flag (above) was adopted as California's official state flag. By that point, however, few grizzlies remained. The last known Yosemite grizzly was shot in 1895, and the last known California grizzly was killed in Sequoia National Forest in 1922.

Although a handful of forest researchers concluded that fire was beneficial and necessary, their work did not influence government policy. But by the 1950s and '60s, the negative effects of fire suppression became undeniable. According to one government report, "Today, much of the west slope [of the Sierra] is a dog-hair thicket of young pines, white fir, and incense cedar, and mature brush—a direct function of overprotection from natural fires."

The overgrown forests had reduced habitat for many animals, and the new vegetation consumed enormous amounts of water, reducing stream flows and lowering water tables. Perhaps most alarming, the new growth had the potential to fuel massive fires that could destroy mature trees. Sierra Nevada forests were, quite literally, sitting on a tinderbox.

Starting in the late 1960s, government officials authorized a regiment of closely monitored prescribed burns in Sierra Nevada forests. The burns duplicated the small natural fires of the past, reduced fire hazards, diversified habitat, returned nutrients to the soil, and allowed fire-adapted plants to regrow. The burns were a success, and in 1968 the National Park Service authorized prescribed burns in Yosemite and Sequoia National Park.

Today prescribed burns are an important part of returning Sierra Nevada forests to their natural state. Burns are conducted only when conditions are safe, and they are closely monitored. The park service also allows natural, lightning-caused fires to burn, although they are closely monitored to ensure that they don't grow out of control. Unfortunately, it will take decades for Sierra Nevada forests to recover. When the damage inflicted by fire suppression has finally been minimized, natural fires will once again maintain the landscape.

Disruption of the Sierra Nevada's natural fire patterns is the most dramatic change wrought by European settlers, but the ecosystem has also been altered in less obvious ways. When white settlers first arrived in Yosemite in the mid-1800s, there were no fish above 6,000 feet due to natural barriers such as waterfalls and steep gradients. In the late 1800s, trout and other non-native fish were introduced to dozens of lakes in Yosemite. In the early days, fish were placed in ten-gallon milk cans and hauled up the mountains by mule. Later, they were dropped from planes into mountain lakes.

Introduced fish made tasty meals for anglers, but they disrupted native ecosystems. The populations of many amphibian species declined as the new arrivals feasted on frogs and tadpoles. Although fish stocking in Yosemite was halted in the 1980s, trout continue to thrive in many high altitude lakes, and amphibian populations continue to decline. A recent drop in mountain yellow-legged frog populations has also been attributed to the deadly chytrid fungus, which has been linked to declining amphibian populations worldwide.

Prescribed Burn

YOSEMITE WILDFLOWERS

Harlequin Lupine
Lupinus stiversii

Mountain Pride Penstemon
Penstemon newberryi

Small Leopard Lily
Lilium parvum

Wild Iris
Iris missouriensis

Pink Monkey Flower
Mimulus lewisii

Coville's Columbine
Aquilegia pubescens

YOSEMITE WILDFLOWERS

Little Elephants Head
Pedicularis attolens

Shooting Star
Dodecatheon jeffreyi

Sierra Rein Orchid
Habenaria dilatata

Mariposa Lily
Calochortus leichtlinii

Indian Paintbrush
Castilleja miniata

Rockfringe
Epilobium obcordatum

VEGETATIVE ZONES

FOOTHILL WOODLANDS (500 - 3,000 feet)

The foothill woodlands, found only at Yosemite's lowest elevations, are hot and dry in summer. Winter brings little or no snow. Common plants include manzanita, interior live oak, Douglas oak, gray pine and many drought-resistant shrubs collectively called chaparral. (The word chaparral is derived from the Spanish *chaparro* "scrub oak.") The foothill woodlands are well adapted to natural fire, passing through frequent cycles of burning and regrowth.

LOWER MONTANE FOREST (3,000 - 6,000 feet)

Lower montane forests cover 166,000 acres in Yosemite, including Yosemite Valley, Wawona and Big Oak Flat Road. This zone experiences hot, dry summers and cool winters that often bring several feet of snow. Dry slopes are dominated by ponderosa pine, while wet slopes harbor white fir. Other species include sugar pine, incense cedar, black oak and giant sequoia. Frequent natural fires historically favored the development of ponderosa-dominated forests throughout the lower montane zone.

UPPER MONTANE FOREST (6,000 - 8,000 feet)

This zone, which covers 216,000 acres in Yosemite, is characterized by cool summers and cold, snowy winters. Typical trees include pure stands of red fir and lodgepole pine. Other species include western juniper and Jeffrey pine (which has bark that smells like vanilla or butterscotch). The upper montane forest is also noteworthy for its gorgeous meadows, which fill with blooming wildflowers between June and August.

SUBALPINE SIERRA NEVADA (8,000 - 10,400 feet)

This is Yosemite's largest vegetative zone, covering 297,000 acres. It's also the official start of the High Sierra, defined as the region above 8,000 feet. The subalpine zone is characterized by short, cool summers and long, snowy winters. Tree species include lodgepole pine, mountain hemlock, western white pine and white bark pine. Lightning strikes are common, but large fires are rare due to the short fire season and frequent natural fire breaks such as meadows and rock outcrops.

ALPINE SIERRA NEVADA (10,400 - 13,000 feet)

Covering 54,300 acres above treeline in Yosemite, the alpine Sierra Nevada is a harsh, rocky landscape where snow covers the ground for most of the year. Summer is measured in weeks, and only hardy plants flourish during the brief growing season. Compared to other alpine areas of comparable latitude in North America, the Sierra Nevada alpine zone is drier than most in the summer, wetter than most in the winter, and warmer than most throughout the year.

COMMON TREES

PONDEROSA PINE
(Pinus ponderosa)
Ponderosa pines are the most common western conifer, with a distribution that roughly outlines the American West. In the central Sierra Nevada they grow at elevations between 3,000 and 6,000 feet. Mature trees can attain heights of 225 feet. Needles grow in bunches of three. The ponderosa's defining characteristic is its pale yellowish bark, which forms large interlocking plates that look like pieces of a jigsaw puzzle.

INCENSE CEDAR
(Calocedrus decurrens)

Incense cedars, distinguished by their thick, stringy bark, grow up to 150 feet tall. Needles are small, flat and waxy. The tree's fragrant wood is often used in pencils. A highly versatile conifer, incense cedars can germinate and grow in both sunny and shady areas. Although once scarce in Yosemite Valley, several decades of fire suppression have allowed incense cedars to flourish.

LODGEPOLE PINE
(Pinus contorta)
Lodgepole pines (named by Lewis & Clark, who observed native tribes using them to build lodges) grow up to 125 feet high. Needles grow in bunches of two. Lodgepoles generally grow between 6,000 and 10,000 feet in the central Sierra Nevada, but occasionally they are found at lower elevations, including Yosemite Valley. The tree's cornflake-like bark is among the thinnest of any pine.

Giant Sequoia

Sequoiadendron giganteum

Even in a park filled with superlatives, giant sequoias *(sequoiadendron giganteum)* remain an unforgettable sight. Weighing two million pounds or more, these gargantuan trees are not just the largest organisms on earth, they are the largest organisms that have *ever* lived on earth. The largest known giant sequoia has a volume of 52,000 cubic feet—ten times the size of a blue whale—and a base over 100 feet in circumference.

Giant sequoias grow on the western slope of California's Sierra Nevada Mountains. Their native range, which is just 260 miles long by 15 miles wide, contains 75 known groves. Yosemite is home to three groves— Mariposa Grove (p.298), Tuolumne Grove (p.224), and Merced Grove (p.217)—which shelter hundreds of mature trees. Reaching a maximum height of 320 feet, giant sequoias are not the tallest trees in the world. That distinction belongs to coast redwoods (*Sequoia sempervirens*), which grow up to 370 feet tall in California and Oregon. Both giant sequoias and coast redwoods belong to the redwood family. A third redwood species, the dawn redwood (*Metasequoia glyptostroboides*), grows in China. Redwoods first appeared roughly 150 million years ago, during the warmer, wetter Jurassic Period, when the trees proliferated across North America, Europe, and Asia. Eventually, as the global climate cooled and dried out, redwoods retreated to their current locations.

Giant sequoias can live up to 3,500 years. Virtually imperishable, mature trees are immune to almost all known pests and diseases. The most common cause of death is toppling over during storms. Although a mature tree's thick, spongy bark can survive most fires, the green crown remains vulnerable. Up to 90 percent of the crown can burn, however, and a giant sequoia will continue to grow.

Far from being destructive, forest fires are beneficial to giant sequoias. Regular fires clear out competing tree species, return nutrients to the soil, and dry out sequoia cones, which causes them to release seeds. Each year mature sequoias produce up to 1,500 cones with about 200 seeds each. Tiny "wings" on the oatmeal-sized seeds maximize wind dispersal, greatly increasing their chances of finding a suitable place to germinate. But the odds of a seed growing into an adult tree are exceptionally slim. Seedlings prefer recently burned soil, plenty of sunshine, and abundant water. Even if all those conditions are present, over 99 percent of seedlings die within their first two years. Seedlings that survive grow tall and pointy for the first 100 years, then develop a rounded crown over the next few centuries. As sequoias grow taller, newer higher branches shade out older lower branches, which die and fall away.

Giant sequoias reach maximum height around 800 years of age, at which point they grow outward and add bulk. Mature sequoias have broad root systems that can reach over 100 feet laterally from the trunk. But, surprisingly, sequoia roots are often less than eight feet deep. In addition to creating a strong foundation for the heavy trees, extensive root systems provide sequoias with water and nutrients. Scientists estimate that the largest sequoias require over 500 gallons of water each day.

■ Giant Sequoias
■ Coast Redwoods

The name "sequoia" was bestowed by Austrian botanist Stephan L. Endlicher when he classified the trees in 1847. Some say the name sequoia was given in honor of a Cherokee man named Sequoyah, who developed a written version of his people's language. Others believe "sequoia" was derived from the Latin word *sequor* ("following") because the enormous trees follow the same classification sequence of other conifers. Before the arrival of Europeans, native tribes called the giant trees *wah-wo-nah* (also written as *wawona*). *Wah-wo-nah* may be an imitation of the great horned owl, which is considered the guardian spirit of these extraordinary trees.

Steller's Jay

Cyanocitta stelleri

These lovely blue birds are common in Yosemite—especially when food is present, as any picnic lover can attest. Steller's jays range from Alaska to Nicaragua. In the western U.S. they are normally found at high elevations. Closely related to blue jays, Steller's jays are distinguished by black heads and black upper bodies. Their call is a harsh, descending *shaaaar*. Steller's jays also imitate the cries of predators such as red-tailed hawks, a trick they use to scare away other birds from feeding areas. Along with crows and magpies, jays are considered among the world's most intelligent birds. In autumn Steller's jays harvest up to 400 acorns per hour. They also eat pine nuts, fruits, seeds, insects, bird eggs—even young birds. They are preyed upon, in turn, by goshawks, which snatch them with vice-like talons. Steller's jays, which typically gather in flocks of ten or more, live in Yosemite year-round. They are named after the German naturalist Georg Steller, who first recorded them in 1741.

Peregrine Falcon

Falco peregrinus

Peregrine falcons are legendary hunters that can spot birds from thousands of feet above, then dive-bomb them at speeds topping 200 mph—the fastest speed of any animal. The collision creates an explosion of feathers. Victims that don't die upon impact have their necks broken by the peregrine's powerful beak. Peregrine falcons are such successful strikers they were used to kill Nazi carrier pigeons in World War II. By the early 1970s, however, U.S. populations had plummeted due to the toxic effects of the pesticide DDT. To save the remaining birds, young peregrines were captured and bred in captivity, then reintroduced into the wild. Peregrines nest on tall cliffs in Yosemite, and from February to August several cliffs are off limits to rock climbers to protect nesting falcons. Adult peregrines have a wingspan up to 3.9 feet. In 1999 peregrine falcons were removed from the federal endangered species list, and in 2009 they were removed from California's endangered species list.

Western Tanager

Piranga ludoviciana

Members of the cardinal family, western tanagers are famous for the male's vibrant breeding plumage. During breeding season the males' bright red face and yellow breast draw a brilliant contrast against its dark black wings. Females are far less showy, with a drab olive coloration. Like all cardinals western tanagers are classified as songbirds. Their call has been described as a hoarse, monotonous *pit-er-ick.* Their summer breeding range, which extends from Alaska to Mexico, covers much of western North America. Western tanagers build flimsy cup nests in which they typically lay four bluish-green eggs with brown spots. Their nests are preyed upon by Clark's nutcrackers and Steller's jays, and adult tanagers are preyed upon by hawks and falcons. The western tanager's winter range extends from central Mexico to Costa Rica, where they are often seen in coffee plantations. Sometimes they migrate alone, sometimes they migrate in groups of up to 30 birds. The majority of their diet consists of insects, but they also feed on berries and fruits.

Great Gray Owl

Strix nebulosa

Great gray owls are the largest owls in North America and the world's largest owl species by length, measuring up to 33 inches long. Their wingspan measures up to five feet across. Due to their large size great gray owls have few natural predators. Their prey consists mostly of small rodents such as voles and shrews. In winter great gray owls use exceptional hearing to detect animals burrowing under snow, then "snow-plunge" their prey. Rather than build their own nests, great gray owls often use the abandoned nests of large birds such as raptors. Although the vast majority of great gray owls live in Canada and Russia, an isolated population of 200-300 owls lives in the Sierra Nevada. This genetically distinct subspecies, *Strix nebulosa Yosemitensis*, is listed as an endangered species in California. Roughly 65 percent of California's great gray owls reside in Yosemite National Park, which marks the southern limit of their range.

Black Bear

Ursus americanus

No animal in Yosemite is as famous, or infamous, as black bears. Their large size, sharp claws, and powerful limbs conjure feelings of fear and dread in many visitors, but black bears are actually quite docile. Unless threatened or provoked—or offered the opportunity to steal human food from cars or tents—black bears generally keep to themselves. No one has ever been killed by a black bear in Yosemite. In fact, far more visitors are injured by deer than bears.

There are roughly 22,000 black bears in California and 400 black bears in Yosemite. Despite their name, California black bears are generally dark brown or cinnamon colored. Their name comes from black bears in the eastern U.S. and the Pacific Northwest, where the bears sport a dark black coat. Yosemite black bears' light coloration leads some visitors to mistake them for grizzly bears, which are also brown. Although grizzly bears historically roamed California, they were eliminated by hunters nearly a century ago (p.65).

Of North America's three bear species—black, grizzly and polar—black bears are the smallest and most common. They grow up to five feet long and three feet high at the shoulder. Yosemite black bears generally weigh between 200 and 350 pounds. The largest bear ever captured in the park weighed 690 pounds. Despite their chubby appearance, black bears are extremely fast, reaching top speeds of 30 mph over short distances. They are also excellent tree climbers.

Black bears are omnivores that eat just about anything, with a preference for grass in spring, berries in summer, and acorns in autumn. Roughly 80 percent of their diet is vegetation, but they also eat ants, termites and insect larvae. In autumn black bears consume up to 20,000 calories per day in preparation for "hibernation." But black bears are not true hibernators. After snuggling into their dens in October or November, they enter a "light" hibernation referred to as Seasonal Lethargy. During this time a black bear's heartbeat drops from roughly 70 beats per minute to as low as eight beats per minute. Compared to true hibernators, a black bear's body temperature drops relatively little. During winter dormancy, which lasts three to five months, black bears lose roughly 25–30 percent of their body weight.

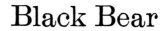

Black Bear Range

Black bears live about 18 years in the wild. The oldest known black bear in Yosemite was

32 years old. Between the ages of three and five, female bears produce their first offspring, then breed about every two years after that. Mating occurs in summer, but embryos do not develop until the mother gains adequate weight to survive winter. Cubs, which weigh less than a pound at birth, are born in late January or early February while the mother is still resting in her den. Most litters consist of one to three cubs, and young bears stay with their mother for a full year while they learn to fend for themselves.

Black bears have relatively poor eyesight, but they have exceptionally good hearing and smell, and they are highly intelligent and adaptable. Unfortunately, some Yosemite black bears have changed their natural behavior in response to a new delicacy: human food. The problem began in the 1920s, when Yosemite's bears discovered the pleasure of eating garbage. Instead of discouraging this behavior, the park established an open air dump where the bears could feast. They then installed bleachers and stadium lighting so visitors could watch the nightly "Bear Show."

Bear Shows ended in 1940, but black bears continued their search for human food. As more people visited Yosemite, conflicts between bears and people grew increasingly common. Bears that repeatedly raided food from cars and tents were deemed "corrupted," and corrupted bears were killed. Before long, hundreds of bears had been killed in Yosemite.

Starting in the 1970s, the park service tried a new approach. Rather than trying to manage bear behavior, they tried to manage human behavior. "Bear-proof" trash cans and food lockers were placed throughout the park, and visitors were handed pamphlets with instructions on proper food storage. Although these efforts have been successful, improper food storage by visitors remains the biggest cause of human-bear conflicts in the park. (For more info on proper food storage, see p.20).

Mule Deer

Odocoileus hemionus

Mule deer are a common sight in Yosemite, often seen grazing in meadows in the early morning or late afternoon. Mule deer are named for their large ears, which move independently of one another like the ears of a mule. Common throughout the West, their range extends from western Canada to central Mexico. Females (does) weigh 95 to 200 pounds, while males (bucks) weigh 150 to 300 pounds.

Mule deer are slightly larger than white-tailed deer, to which they are closely related. Mule deer have white tails with a black tip, and their bifurcated antlers "fork" as they grow. (The antlers of white-tailed deer, by contrast, branch from a single main beam.) Bucks grow a large pair of antlers each year, then shed them each winter. This annual cycle of antler growth is regulated by changes in the length of the day.

Bucks compete for females during the fall rut, enmeshing their antlers and trying to force the head of their competitors down. Injuries are rare, but antlers sometimes become locked together. If two enmeshed bucks cannot unlock their antlers, both will eventually die of starvation.

After breeding in autumn, gestation lasts 190 to 200 days. Young does give birth to one fawn. Older does often give birth to twins. Fawns are born with white spots to help camouflage them with the dappled light of the forest floor, but as fawns grow older the spots disappear. Fawns can identify their mother through a unique odor produced by glands on the mother's hind legs. Fawns stay with their mothers until they are weaned in the fall. Conflict between does is common, so family groups are often spaced widely apart.

Mule deer are ruminants that ferment plants in their multi-chamber stomach before digestion. In summer they forage on plants, leaves and brushy vegetation. In winter they forage on conifers such as ponderosa pine. Gray winter fur is replaced in spring with a brown summer coat. Adult mule deer can live 11 years or more in the wild, but only if they avoid predators such as mountain lions, bobcats and coyotes.

Mule Deer
Range

Mountain Lion
Felis concolor

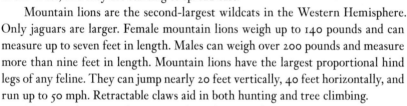

Mountain lions (also called cougars, pumas, panthers and catamounts) are found from Canada to Argentina—the most extensive range of any mammal in the Western Hemisphere. Before European settlement, mountain lions inhabited all 48 lower U.S. states, but in the late 1800s and early 1900s they were hunted to the brink of extinction. Following the enactment of strict hunting regulations, mountain lions have made a steady comeback in the West, and they are starting to spread east.

Mountain lions are the second-largest wildcats in the Western Hemisphere. Only jaguars are larger. Female mountain lions weigh up to 140 pounds and can measure up to seven feet in length. Males can weigh over 200 pounds and measure more than nine feet in length. Mountain lions have the largest proportional hind legs of any feline. They can jump nearly 20 feet vertically, 40 feet horizontally, and run up to 50 mph. Retractable claws aid in both hunting and tree climbing.

Mountain lions travel up to 25 miles a day in search of food, killing prey every four to eight days. Excellent night vision enables them to hunt from dusk till dawn. They are quick, efficient hunters that quietly stalk prey before pouncing. Victims often die from a lethal bite to the spinal cord. In Yosemite mountain lions hunt mule deer and bighorn sheep, but much of their diet consists of smaller animals like squirrels and rodents.

Solitary and territorial, mountain lions prefer an extensive home range of up to 300 square miles. Adult mountain lions come together only to mate. Females are solely responsible for parenting, and cubs stay with mothers for roughly two years while learning survival skills. Mountain lion pups are born with spots, but they develop a uniform tan coloration by about 2.5 years in age.

Reclusive by nature, mountain lions go to great lengths to avoid people. Sightings are extremely rare, and there has never been a fatal human attack in Yosemite. If you do encounter a mountain lion, slowly back away while holding a steady gaze.

Mountain Lion Range

Coyote
Canis latrans

Coyotes are often elusive during the day, but their haunting howls echo through Yosemite at night. One long, high-pitched howl calls a pack together, and when the pack has gathered a series of yips and yelps are often added to the mix. Coyotes have a reputation as tricksters, however, and what sounds like a large pack is sometimes just one or two coyotes making a variety of sounds to create the auditory illusion of a larger pack. Coyote vocalizations are surprisingly complex, with up to 11 distinct howls, yips, yaps and barks to communicate with one another.

Coyotes currently range from Canada to Panama, but historically they were confined to the open spaces of the Western U.S. and Mexico. Following the extermination of wolves in the 1800s, coyotes spread rapidly throughout North America. Intelligent, adaptable animals with a knack for scavenging, coyote populations have held steady and even increased in some places despite years of being hunted, poisoned and trapped. This is partly due to a remarkable reproductive adaptation: when coyote populations decline, the remaining coyotes produce large litters.

Coyotes often travel in packs of six or so closely related family members. Their diet consists mostly of small mammals such as mice, squirrels and rabbits. Coyotes are highly opportunistic, however, and they will eat just about anything, including birds, snakes, insects and trash. Working in teams, coyotes sometimes hunt larger animals such as mule deer. While pursuing prey, they can reach top speeds of over 40 mph and jump 13 feet in length.

Coyotes mate in winter, and mothers give birth to an average of six pups in spring. Young coyotes are extremely vulnerable, and up to two-thirds of pups do not survive to adulthood. Those that survive their first year can often live ten years or more in the wild. Adult coyotes grow up to four feet in length and weigh up to 40 pounds. In Yosemite mountain lions are coyotes' only natural predator.

Coyote Range

Coyotes play a central role in the myths and legends of many native tribes. Among a cast of human/animal characters, Coyote is often portrayed as an intelligent, scheming trickster. The word "coyote" is derived from the Aztec word *cóyotl*. Coyote's Latin name, *Canis latrans*, means "barking dog."

Bighorn Sheep

Ovis canadensis

Bighorn sheep are among Yosemite's most impressive animals. Well adapted to alpine terrain, they can traverse narrow ledges, scramble up steep slopes, and jump down 20-foot inclines with grace. Their unique concave hooves, which feature a hard outer edge and soft interior sole, help them grip rocks and navigate cliffs. John Muir called bighorn sheep "the bravest of all the Sierra mountaineers."

The ram's legendary horns take up to a decade to grow, curving up and over the ears in a C-shaped curl. A large pair of horns can weigh up to 30 pounds and reach 30 inches in length. During mating season, competing rams charge each other head-on at speeds topping 20 mph. When rams collide, their horns smash together, producing a loud cracking sound that can be heard for miles. Thickened skulls allow rams to withstand repeated collisions. Some rams fight for over 24 hours, and those with the biggest horns generally do the most mating.

Bighorn rams weigh up to 220 pounds. Ewes weigh up to 160 pounds. Both rams and ewes develop horns shortly after birth, but ewe horns are skinny and never grow past half curl. Ewes generally stay with their family herd. Adult rams, by contrast, live largely isolated lives. In the Sierra Nevada, bighorn sheep live at elevations between 10,000 and 14,000 feet.

Sierra Nevada bighorn sheep (*Ovis canadensis sierrae*) are one of three bighorn subspecies. The other two are Rocky Mountain bighorn sheep and Desert bighorn sheep. Prior to European settlement, several thousand bighorn sheep roamed the Sierra Nevada Mountains. By 1979, however, the Sierra bighorn population had fallen to barely 100 animals due to hunting and diseases transmitted from domestic sheep. In the 1980s a bighorn recovery program established several new herds, including one in Yosemite's Cathedral Range. Today there are roughly 600 bighorn sheep in the Sierra Nevada Mountains.

Bighorn Sheep Range

Yellow-Bellied Marmot

Marmota flaviventris

These roly-poly alpine critters are one of the High Sierra's most lovable sights. Western cousins of *Marmota monax* (better known as groundhogs or woodchucks) marmots are often seen perched high on a rock, taking in their surroundings or basking in the summer sun. Marmots generally live above 6,500 feet in the western U.S. and Canada, and they are common in the Sierra Nevada.

Despite their yellow-bellied name, marmots won't think twice about grabbing your lunch. During the short summer season marmots are aggressive food opportunists, eating as much as possible and packing on thick layers of fat to survive the harsh winter ahead. Their diet includes leaves, grasses, berries, flowers, insects, and bird eggs. By the time autumn rolls around, male marmots, which are larger than females, can weigh up to 11.5 pounds.

Marmots are deep hibernators, spending up to eight months in hibernation in dens up to 23 feet deep. During this time their metabolic rate slows by as much as two-thirds. Their body temperature drops from 97°F to 40°F, their heartbeat drops from 100 beats per minute to four beats per minute, and they only breathe once every six minutes.

After emerging from hibernation dens in spring, male marmots dig new, smaller dens under rock piles. The new den, which typically measures three feet deep, keeps them safe from predators such as mountain lions and coyotes. Each male then gathers a harem of up to four females to live in his den. Marmots have a "harem-polygynous" mating system where a male defends multiple females. Marmots form colonies of ten to 20 individuals. When one marmot spots a predator, it emits a loud whistle to warn other marmots of the danger at hand.

Marmot Range

Female marmots have litters of three to five pups, but only about half of those pups survive their first year. Young females typically remain in their home area, while yearling males venture out in search of available females. Marmots reproduce around two years of age, and adult marmots can live up to 15 years.

Little Brown Bat

Myotis lucifugus

Little brown bats are one of 17 bat species found in Yosemite. Their wingspans measure up to 10.5 inches wide, yet they weigh just 0.5 ounces. Like all bats they use echolocation, a technique similar to radar, to find insects such as wasps and mosquitos. While in flight little brown bats emit 20 high-pitched calls per second, but when closing in on prey they emit up to 200 calls per second. These calls, which have a frequency of 40-80 kHz, are beyond the range of human hearing. Little brown bats use their wings to scoop bugs into their mouths, and a single bat can consume up to 1,200 insects each night. Little brown bats undergo a daily "torpor," or sleep state, which can last up to 20 hours. They are most active at dusk and dawn. In summer, males and females live apart while females raise the young. In winter, both sexes migrate south to hibernate together.

Belding's Ground Squirrel

Spermophilus beldingi

These adorable ground squirrels live in alpine meadows above 5,000 feet. When not nibbling on grasses and flowers, they often sit erect on their haunches, earning them the nickname "picket pin" squirrel. Belding's ground squirrels hibernate seven to eight months—one of the longest hibernation periods of any mammal in North America. To prepare for their long hibernation, Belding's ground squirrels eat voraciously throughout summer, doubling their weight by autumn and increasing their body fat by a factor of 15. Males emerge from hibernation about two weeks before females, tunneling through snow to reach the surface. Females emerge when the snow has melted. Within six days females are ready to mate, but they will only mate on a single day during a window that lasts just three to six hours. Not surprisingly, competition for females is fierce. Fighting among males is common, and injuries can be fatal. Females mate with several males, then give birth to a litter about one month later. By late August male pups have moved away from their birthplace. Females stay where they were born, and multiple female generations often share an ancestral site.

HISTORY

THE FIRST PEOPLE in Yosemite were the Miwok tribe, who lived in the central Sierra Nevada for thousands of years. To the Miwok, Yosemite Valley was paradise on earth: a fortress-like hideaway filled with fresh water, edible plants and wild game. They called the valley *Ahwahnee*, "Place Like A Gaping Mouth," and they called themselves *Ahwahneechee*, "People of the Ahwahnee."

Yosemite Valley's abundant natural resources supported roughly 200 Ahwahneechee—a fraction of the estimated 100,000 people living in the Sierra Nevada, but relatively large for a single location. Over 35 Ahwahneechee living sites have been identified in Yosemite Valley, including permanent villages and seasonal hunting and fishing camps. The largest and most important village, *Koomine*, stretched roughly three-quarters of a mile below Yosemite Falls.

During the hot summer months the Ahwahneechee wore few clothes. Men covered themselves with a single piece of deerskin folded about the hips, women wore a two-piece buckskin skirt, and children were largely naked until about ten years of age. Important villagers wore buckskin sashes and decorated their hair with wildflowers. When temperatures dropped, the Ahwahneechee wrapped themselves in animal-skin robes. Although they often went barefoot during the warmer months, the Ahwahneechee wore cedar bark-lined moccasins in winter. Snowshoes, fashioned out of split saplings, aided winter travel in the High Sierra.

Edible plants gathered by Ahwahneechee women made up most of the tribe's diet. Greens and bulbs were harvested in spring, seeds and fruits in summer, and acorns in fall. All told, over 100 plant species were harvested. In bountiful years excess crops were dried and placed in storage. In lean years the Ahwahneechee turned to alternate crops and traded for food with neighboring tribes, including the Mono, Yokuts, and Midou. In exchange for Ahwahneechee acorns, berries, baskets and arrow shafts, neighboring tribes traded salt, piñon pine nuts, red pigment for paint, and obsidian (volcanic glass) for arrowheads.

Acorns and other wild crops were the tribe's main sources of food, but they also hunted wild animals. Hunting was the responsibility of Ahwahneechee males, who often wore a disguise when hunting. The most impressive disguise was the entire skin of a buck, complete with antler-shaped twigs, wrapped around the hunter's body. This disguise was believed to hold magical powers, and it was put on in secret and kept hidden between hunting ceremonies to avoid contamination by women and children. In the field, the disguised hunter mimicked deer movements until he was accepted by a herd.

In their free time, both men and women played a sport similar to lacrosse with basket rackets and a buckskin ball shot through willow goal posts. Villagers also gambled on archery tournaments, footraces and spear-throwing contests. Ceremonies and rituals were common throughout the year. Special "world-renewing ceremonies" were held in spring and fall to bring rain, maintain bountiful crops, provide animals for hunting, and prevent natural disasters.

According to early Yosemite settler Galen Clark, the Ahwahneechee were polygamists. Women were considered property, and parents sold young daughters to the highest suitable bidder. Payment for a bride was considered an important part of the marriage ceremony. Wealthy men often had two or three wives, and husbands could sell or gamble their wives away—though such occurrences were said to be rare. If a woman was unfaithful to her husband, she was punished with death.

Although generally peaceful, the Ahwahneechee occasionally fought with neighboring tribes. Galen Clark described them as "perhaps the most warlike of any of the tribes in this part of the Sierra Nevada Mountains, who were, as a rule, a peaceful people." Most disputes were settled through negotiation, but when negotiation failed tribes resorted to violence.

Ahwahneechee Dwellings

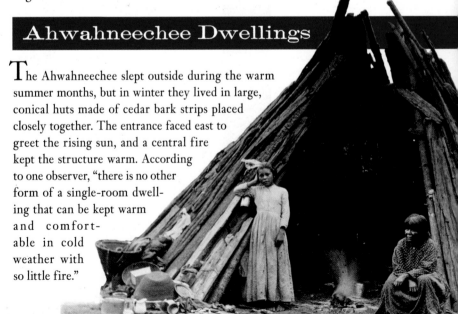

The Ahwahneechee slept outside during the warm summer months, but in winter they lived in large, conical huts made of cedar bark strips placed closely together. The entrance faced east to greet the rising sun, and a central fire kept the structure warm. According to one observer, "there is no other form of a single-room dwelling that can be kept warm and comfortable in cold weather with so little fire."

Ahwahneechee Basketry

Basket making was one of the most important aspects of Ahwahneechee culture. In the absence of pottery, baskets were essential to daily life. There were dozens of baskets with hundreds of uses: storing food, collecting trash, transporting firewood, trapping fish, etc. Baskets were given as gifts and buried with the dead. Basket making was the exclusive domain of women, and basketry skills helped determine a woman's social status within the tribe. Ahwahneechee women were such skilled weavers that some baskets were watertight.

Serving far more than just practical needs, basketry was a form of self-expression with important symbolic meanings. Ahwahneechee women wove beautiful baskets decorated with beads and feathers, and top basket makers were as dexterous as professional musicians. Many women continued weaving into old age long after their eyesight failed. Basketry was a combination of technical skill and encyclopedic botanical knowledge. Plants left to grow wild produced inferior weaving products, so Indians cultivated plants through burning and pruning to produce the longest, straightest fibers. The quality of fibers also depended on the timing of the harvest. This extensive botanical knowledge, learned and mastered over thousands of years, was passed down each generation from mother to daughter.

Basket making was a full-blown industry in the Sierra Nevada. Roughly 50 percent of all harvested plants were used to make baskets. Large, complex baskets often required thousands of shoots, and over the course of a year an entire village might require hundreds of thousands of shoots from various plants. Such demand could only be satisfied through large-scale harvesting. Most basketry materials also required prolonged storage of one to three years to properly season the fibers, which meant weavers had to plan their basketry needs several years in advance.

EUROPEAN DISCOVERY

IN 1542 JUAN Rodríguez Cabrillo sailed north from Mexico to become the first non-native to explore California. Just south of present-day Monterey, Cabrillo spied snow-capped mountains in the distance and described them as *la sierra nevada*, "the snowy mountains." But the mountains he saw were not the present-day Sierra Nevada, which has led to much confusion regarding the history of the range. It wasn't until 1776 that Pedro Font, a Spaniard who helped colonize San Francisco, saw the present-day Sierra Nevada Mountains and described them as *una gran sierra nevada*, "great snowy mountains." That same year he produced a map of the region and labeled the mountains "Sierra Nevada."

For the next five decades, the Sierra Nevada were essentially ignored. As far as the Spanish were concerned, the range was little more than a barrier to eastern travel, and they already had their hands full along the coast. Not only were their Catholic missions in disarray, but Mexico was threatening to revolt.

Following the Mexican War of Independence (1810-1821), Mexico expelled Spain and gained control of California. Around the same time American beaver trappers ventured into California from the east. In 1827 legendary fur trapper Jedediah Smith, fresh from blazing an overland route from the Rocky Mountains to Southern California, led two companions up and over the western slope of the Sierra Nevada. Just 27 years old, Smith became the first white man to cross the rugged mountains, trudging through deep snow just north of Yosemite.

Seven years later, the U.S. Army dispatched a 58-man expedition to cross the Sierra Nevada from the east. Led by 34-year-old Joseph Walker—a man whose "chief delight" was "to explore unknown regions"—the expedition hoped to gather basic information about California. In mid-October 1833, after leading his men across the Great Basin Desert, Joseph Walker reached the eastern base of the Sierra Nevada. By the time he arrived, however, the mountains were covered in snow.

Undaunted, the men climbed the Sierra Nevada's sheer eastern slope. It was a grueling journey. Deep snow slowed their progress, and foraging was virtually impossible for the expedition's pack animals. The men, dressed in knee-length buckskin shirts and leather leggings, battled frostbite and starvation. Through sheer determination they reached the crest of the Sierra Nevada, then began the long descent down the western slope. As food supplies dwindled, the men were reduced to eating horses that died along the way. "Our situation was growing more distressing every hour," one party member wrote, "and all we now thought of was to extricate ourselves from this inhospitable region."

Pushing on, the men followed a large stream they hoped would lead them to the base of the mountains. After a short distance the stream burst through the forest and plunged over the edge of a sheer cliff. Standing on a rocky precipice, they became the first white men to set eyes on Yosemite Valley.

Pulling out a spyglass, Walker scanned the surroundings. Yosemite Valley was free of snow and in full autumn glory. Sheer cliffs, granite domes, and dramatic waterfalls towered above open forests and meadows. A sparkling river twisted through the center of the valley. To the shivering, half-starved men, it seemed like divine intervention—the perfect place to hunt and graze their pack animals. For two days the men tried to find a feasible route down the sheer cliffs, but each time they failed. Eventually they concluded that it was "utterly impossible for a man to descend."

Dejected, the men spent three days bushwhacking an alternate route down the mountains. Although Walker's party never entered Yosemite Valley, the fact that they saw it at all was a minor miracle. Tucked away deep in the heart of the Sierra Nevada Mountains, surrounded on all sides by forests and cliffs, Yosemite Valley is one of the most geographically well-concealed locations in California. In the mid-1800s, you literally had to stumble upon Yosemite Valley to find it—which is exactly what the next white people did.

In October 1849, two gold miners were tracking a grizzly bear just south of Yosemite. Bushwhacking through the trees, the men stumbled upon an Ahwahneechee trail and followed it to the entrance of Yosemite Valley. Laid out before them were "stupendous cliffs rising perhaps 3000 feet from their base which gave us cause for wonder." Content simply to savor the view, the two men never entered Yosemite Valley. Had they ventured farther they would have encountered a world virtually unchanged since the Walker expedition passed by 15 years earlier. In the intervening years, however, life just downhill from Yosemite Valley had forever changed.

THE GOLD RUSH

ON JANUARY 24, 1848, nine days before the U.S. acquired California from Mexico, James Marshall noticed something sparkling in the American River in the foothills northwest of Yosemite. "It made my heart thump," he later recounted, "for I was certain it was gold." Marshall tried to keep his discovery secret, but rumors quickly spread. When local store owner Sam Brannan heard the news, he purchased huge quantities of mining supplies, traveled to San Francisco, and waved a bottle of gold dust over his head shouting, "Gold! Gold from the American River!" Within a few weeks, 75 percent of the men living in San Francisco had left town to search for gold.

News of California's instant riches spread like wildfire across the globe. At the start of 1848, 800 people lived in San Francisco. By the end of 1849, 100,000 people had arrived in California, and thousands more were on their way. They came from Europe, China, Australia, South America—anywhere the news spread. In 1850 California demanded statehood and got it. By the end of the decade, over 300,000 people had flooded into the state and two million pounds of gold (worth roughly $50 billion today) had been pulled out of streams and mines.

In 1848, when miners first arrived in the Sierra foothills, the natives living there greeted them with hospitality. Many watched the mining process with great interest, and when they realized the value of the shiny metal they panned for it themselves. Native tribes eagerly exchanged gold dust for blankets and other supplies. For a short while, everything was fine.

Then, as tens of thousands of miners poured into the foothills, the situation quickly deteriorated. Miners competed with natives for deer and chopped down acorn-bearing oak trees—an important source of food. Many miners were distrustful of the natives and confiscated their territory by force. Within just a few months many people became second-class citizens in a land they had occupied for thousands of years.

Angry and starving, some tribes were reduced to raiding mining camps and trading posts. Such incidents, reported widely among miners, further fueled white suspicion, leading to a downward spiral in relations.

Just south of Yosemite, a ruthless, charismatic man named James Savage employed hundreds of natives to work his lucrative mining claims. A former cattle thief, Savage quickly turned his attention to gold, and before long he oversaw a small empire of gold mines and trading posts. By 1850 he was earning roughly $20,000 a day. To ensure his workers' goodwill, he learned their language, adopted their customs, and married the daughters of chiefs. He also intimidated them through claims of supernatural powers. According to one story, he once let a native man shoot him with a gun filled with six blanks. As each shot went off, Savage made a grabbing gesture in the air. When the smoke cleared, Savage produced six bullets in his hands—proof, he declared, that guns could not harm him.

According to one observer, "Jim Savage was the absolute and despotic ruler over thousands of Indians ... and was by them designated in their Spanish vernacular *El Rey Guero*—the blonde king."

As Savage amassed a small fortune, he grew increasingly flamboyant. His workers, meanwhile, grew increasingly unhappy as they realized he was growing rich at their expense. On a trip to San Francisco with tribal leader José Juarez, Savage visited a gambling hall, jumped up on a table, and bet his weight in gold on a playing card. In an instant he lost $35,000. He paid the debt with money given to him by workers to purchase supplies. Juarez, outraged, berated Savage in the street. Savage responded by knocking Juarez to the ground.

Word of Savage's exploits quickly spread among his workers, and Savage returned home to a flurry of discontent. With the situation spiraling out of control, Savage called several tribal leaders together. Addressing them in their own language, Savage said, "If war is made and the white men are aroused to anger, every Indian engaged in war will be killed."

Juarez, still fuming, stated that white men in faraway cities would not help miners fight Indians. But even if they did, "we will go to the mountains. If they follow, they cannot find us. Our country is now overrun with white people; we must fight to protect ourselves."

THE MARIPOSA BATTALION

IN DECEMBER 1851, two of Savage's trading posts were raided by angry natives. Fearful of reprisal, hundreds of Savage's workers fled to the mountains. In response, Savage assembled a 200-man militia called the Mariposa Battalion, with Savage serving as commander.

Before the battalion could take action, however, federal Indian commissioners arrived and demanded a halt to hostile activities. Hoping for a diplomatic solution, the commissioners tried to negotiate peace treaties with local tribes. In exchange for leaving the mountains, most "hostile" tribes accepted government land in the Central Valley. But the Ahwahneechee refused. White men had yet to enter Yosemite Valley, and the Ahwahneechee had no interest in leaving their home. A stalemate ensued. The Indian commissioners gave the Ahwahneechee eight days to leave the mountains, but they refused to budge. With no solution at hand, the Mariposa Battalion headed to Yosemite Valley.

At the time, the Ahwahneechee were led by a powerful chief named Tenaya, who had only recently led his people back to Yosemite. Several decades earlier, a plague had swept through the mountains, and Yosemite Valley was abandoned. The survivors, including Tenaya's father, fled to the desert at the eastern base of the Sierra Nevada to live with the Mono Indians. Tenaya's father took a Mono wife, but Tenaya was raised listening to stories of the old days in Yosemite Valley. When Tenaya was a young man, an old shaman urged him to leave the desert and reestablish his people in the mountains. Sometime around 1821, Tenaya returned to Yosemite Valley with 200 followers.

Now the Ahwahneechee were confronted with a new threat. As the Mariposa Battalion approached Yosemite Valley, Tenaya headed down to meet Savage. Tenaya asked Savage why his people were being expelled from their homeland. Savage told him the white man would give them everything they needed, including protection.

"We have all we need," Tenaya responded, "we do not want anything from white men … let us remain in the mountains where we were born." Savage was unmoved by the chief's argument. If a treaty is not signed, he told Tenaya, "your whole tribe will be destroyed; not one of them will be left alive."

Torn between expulsion and war, Tenaya reluctantly surrendered. A few days later, the battalion forced roughly 70 Ahwahneechee to trudge out of the mountains through deep snow. But Savage suspected many Ahwahneechee remained, so he continued to Yosemite Valley with roughly 60 battalion members.

On March 27, 1851, the soldiers reached an overlook with breathtaking views of Yosemite Valley. The light was soft and a fine mist swirled through the trees. One man in the party, Dr. Lafayette Bunnell, was moved to tears by the scenery. Savage thought Bunnell foolish and ordered him to move on. Descending towards Bridalveil Fall, they became the first white men to enter Yosemite Valley.

The next day the men searched the valley and found an abandoned village, indicating that the remaining Ahwahneechee had fled to higher elevations. But the battalion, running low on supplies, was forced to turn around. Meanwhile, Tenaya and the other captive Ahwahneechee had somehow managed to escape in the middle of the night. To Savage, the expedition was a failure. But Bunnell would later write: "We had discovered, named, and partially explored, one of the most remarkable … geographical wonders of the world."

A few weeks later, a second expedition headed to Yosemite Valley, rounded up the Ahwahneechee, and marched them to the reservation at gunpoint. But life on the reservation was miserable, and Tenaya pleaded with his captors to let his tribe return to Yosemite Valley. Eventually, they were granted permission to leave, and no effort was made to bring them back.

Then, in 1852, a group of miners wandered into Yosemite Valley to pan for gold. A skirmish broke out that left two miners dead, and another militia was dispatched to Yosemite Valley. Five Ahwahneechee were shot and several more were hung from oak trees. Tenaya, convinced the hostility was far from over, ordered his people to cross the Sierra Nevada and take shelter with the Mono tribe.

The following year, Tenaya led his people back to Yosemite Valley. A few months later, however, a group of young Ahwahneechee supposedly stole horses from the Mono, and the Mono sent a war party to Yosemite Valley in response. In the skirmish that ensued, Tenaya was stoned to death. Many young Ahwahneechee were also killed, and the women and children were taken captive by the Mono and marched across the Sierra Nevada. Only a handful of elderly Ahwahneechee were allowed to remain in Yosemite Valley. From that point forward, traditional Ahwahneechee life would never be the same.

GRIZZLY ADAMS

In 1849 a bankrupt Massachusetts shoemaker named James Adams headed to California to search for gold. After making and losing several fortunes, Adams grew despondent. "I abandoned all my schemes for wealth," he wrote, "and took the road towards the wildest and most unfrequented parts of the Sierra Nevada, resolved to make the wilderness my home, and wild beasts my companions." In 1856 Adams moved to San Francisco and opened The Mountaineer Museum, which featured elk, eagles, vultures, wildcats, mountain lions and trained grizzlies that performed tricks. Holding court was Adams himself, dressed in fringed buckskin, moccasins and a deerskin hat. The museum was a hit, and Adams, who had a knack for publicity, often walked through downtown San Francisco with his grizzly bears in tow. His star attraction, Samson, a 1,500-pound grizzly captured in Yosemite, became the model for California's state flag.

ARTISTS & TOURISTS

AT FIRST, MOST Californians knew nothing of the discovery of Yosemite Valley by the Mariposa Battalion. The foothills were filled with gold, and miners could think of little else. Then, in 1855, a writer named James Hutchings came across a printed account of the battalion's expedition. He could hardly believe what he read. The discovery of a 1,000-foot waterfall—six times higher than world-famous Niagara Falls—was extraordinary news that had yet to be widely reported. Hutchings, who was in the midst of launching an illustrated monthly magazine, decided to visit the mysterious valley.

Hutchings arrived in June with three companions and two native guides. The group spent five days exploring Yosemite Valley, taking notes, sketching illustrations, and basking in the remarkable scenery. Hutchings was beside himself. The glory of Yosemite Valley far exceeded his expectations—the waterfall he read about was, in fact, over 2,000 feet high—and shortly thereafter he wrote a glowing article for a Mariposa newspaper describing the "luxurious scenic banqueting." By the end of that summer, over 40 people had visited Yosemite Valley.

The following year, two enterprising miners opened a 50-mile horse trail to Yosemite Valley, charging $2 per rider. The multi-day ride, which involved steep climbs and sheer drop offs, was enough to deter most visitors, but a few dozen adventure seekers braved the hardship to witness the scenery firsthand. Yosemite Valley's first hotel opened in 1857, followed by an even larger hotel two years later. Both structures consisted of dirt floors, rooms separated by hanging sheets, and windows with no panes. But the incredible scenery and warm hospitality made up for the rustic accommodations.

Halfway along the trail to Yosemite Valley was a large meadow called Wawona, and Galen Clark, one of the first visitors to Yosemite Valley, took up residence there in 1856. Clark built an inn for overnight guests and guided visitors to the Mariposa Grove of giant sequoias. Before long, the "Big Trees" had also become a must-see destination.

As news of Yosemite's extraordinary scenery spread through California, more and more people stopped by for a look. Artists were among the earliest arrivals, and their photos, paintings, and illustrations further fueled public curiosity. In 1861 the influential Reverand Thomas Starr King visited Yosemite Valley. When he returned to San Francisco, he preached its wonders from his pulpit and wrote glowing articles that reached a national audience.

That same year, James Hutchings published *Scenes of Wonder and Curiosity in California*, an illustrated book that lavished praise upon Yosemite. To Hutchings, who would soon purchase a hotel in the valley, Yosemite was an underexploited scenic gold mine. But as hoteliers and settlers snatched up plots of land, some visitors grew concerned at the pace of unchecked development.

Guardian of Yosemite
GALEN CLARK

In 1855 Galen Clark visited Yosemite Valley as a member of the second tourist party. Several months later he developed serious lung problems. Told he had a short time to live, Clark, 42, moved to present-day Wawona. "I went to the mountains," he wrote, "to take my chances of dying or growing better which I thought were about even." Shortly thereafter, he completely recovered, and Clark spent most of his next 53 years living in Yosemite.

Born in Dublin, New Hampshire, in 1814, Clark was a polite, sickly child who attained little success as a young man. At age 38 he was broke and living in New York City when he saw an exhibition displaying gold dust from California. Enchanted, he set sail for the West Coast and sought work as a miner.

After developing lung problems, Clark claimed 160 acres in Wawona and built a small cabin in the meadow. Awed by the size of the giant sequoias in nearby Mariposa Grove, Clark wasted no time publicizing the "Big Trees" in local newspapers. Before long he was hosting paying guests at his cabin and leading them on guided tours of the Mariposa Grove. The Reverend Thomas Starr King called Clark "one of the best informed men, one of the very best guides, I ever met in California or any other wilderness." Another guest described him as "handsome, thoughtful, interesting, and slovenly."

Although generally well-liked, Clark had many unusual habits. He frequently walked barefoot, claiming that shoes and boots were "cruel and silly instruments of torture, at once uncivilized, inhuman, and unnecessary." Clark also insisted on breathing through his nose while he hiked. "As the air rushes through the nostrils on its way to inflate the lungs," he explained, "the brain attracts and inhales electricity from it."

When the Yosemite Grant was created in 1864, Clark was designated the first "Guardian of Yosemite" (a position comparable to park superintendent today). Clark later befriended John Muir and became a charter member of the Sierra Club. Muir described Clark as "the best mountaineer I ever met, and one of the kindest and most amiable of all my mountain friends."

In 1910, 53 years after coming to Yosemite to die, Galen Clark passed away at age 96. He was buried near Yosemite Falls at a spot he had selected decades earlier. His gravesite, marked by a granite tombstone, is surrounded by giant sequoia seedlings that Clark planted. Today, over a century later, those young sequoias continue to grow.

In early 1864, a group of influential citizens approached California Senator John Conness with a novel idea. A place as extraordinary as Yosemite, they argued, should belong to the public, not private landowners. They urged the creation of a state-owned land trust to preserve Yosemite for future generations.

Spearheading the effort was Israel Raymond, a wealthy San Francisco businessman. Raymond sent Conness a letter urging him to transfer Yosemite and the Mariposa Grove from the federal government to the state of California "for public use and recreation." Included with the letter was a set of Yosemite photographs taken by celebrated photographer Carleton Watkins.

By 1864, nearly a decade after James Hutchings first arrived in Yosemite, fewer than 700 tourists had visited Yosemite Valley. But Conness was suitably impressed by the photographs to introduce a bill in Congress. "This bill," he announced, "proposes to make a grant of certain premises located in the Sierra Nevada mountains, in the state of California, that are for all public purposes worthless, but which constitute, perhaps, some of the greatest wonders of the world." To assure the bill's passage, Conness promised his colleagues that it would not cost the federal government a dime. Congress, preoccupied with the Civil War, passed the bill without objection.

On June 30, 1864, President Abraham Lincoln signed what came to be called the Yosemite Grant. Although few people realized it at the time, the Yosemite Grant was a radical achievement unprecedented in human history. Never before had a government set aside a piece of wilderness for its citizens simply because it was beautiful. But this radical idea, which laid the foundation for the creation of America's national parks, soon spread around the world.

Artists in Yosemite

Eadweard Muybridge

Eadweard Muybridge was not the first photographer to visit Yosemite, but he was the first photographer to infuse his Yosemite photographs with romance and drama. He composed his shots like landscape paintings and added embellishing details like clouds. Following his first visit to Yosemite, the English-born Muybridge (birth-name: Edward Muggeridge) adopted the pseudonym "Helios." He then exhibited Helios' photographs in a San Francisco gallery, handing out brochures remarking on the "anonymous" artist's supreme talents. The response was overwhelming. People loved the mystery photographer's dramatic, painterly approach. When it was revealed that Muybridge was Helios, critics were appalled. But the public didn't care, and Muybridge's career continued to thrive.

In 1872, at age 41, Muybridge married his 21-year-old photography assistant. Several years later, convinced she was cheating on him, Muybridge tracked down her supposed lover to a home near Calistoga. When the man opened the door, Muybridge announced "here's the answer to the letter you sent my wife" and shot him at point-blank range. He then apologized to several women present, calmly sat down in the parlor, and began reading a newspaper. Muybridge was ultimately acquitted of murder on the grounds of "justifiable homicide." Around the same time, former California Governor Leland Stanford hired him to settle a bet about whether horses trot with all four feet off the ground. His groundbreaking work photographing galloping horses paved the way for the invention of motion pictures.

Albert Bierstadt

Many painters visited Yosemite in the mid-1800s, but none were as famous or successful as Albert Bierstadt. At the time, landscape painting exhibitions drew blockbuster crowds in major American cities, offering the public a rare glimpse of the American West that few people had the time or the money to visit. Landscape artists were treated like rock stars, and Bierstadt's massive, melodramatic landscapes were among the most popular. A master of self-promotion, he displayed his works as if they were performances: charging admission, unveiling them from behind velvet curtains, lighting them dramatically, and even recommending they be viewed through binoculars to heighten the visual effect.

His first monumental Yosemite painting, *Looking Down Yosemite Valley, California* (above), measured 40 square feet and was unveiled to the public in 1865. The painting established Bierstadt as America's top landscape artist, and the giant canvas toured several major cities. In 1867 a wealthy financier commissioned a massive 140-square-foot Yosemite painting for $25,000. When that painting, *The Domes of Yosemite*, was unveiled to the public, it caused a firestorm of criticism. Some considered it Bierstadt's finest work. Others accused Bierstadt of vulgar exaggeration. The scenery was simply *too* perfect. When Mark Twain viewed the canvas he joked that it was "considerably more beautiful than the original," describing it as "more the atmosphere of Kingdom-Come than of California." Although some critics scoffed, Bierstadt remained one of the most popular and influential landscape artists of the 19th century.

JOHN MUIR

Of all the great artists and thinkers Yosemite has nurtured, none has been more celebrated, more influential, and more romanticized than John Muir. His eloquent nature writing helped inspire the modern environmental movement, and his tireless efforts were vital to the creation of Yosemite National Park.

Born in Scotland in 1838, Muir moved to Wisconsin with his parents when he was a child. His father was a strict Presbyterian preacher who demanded that young John memorize the Bible word for word. Later, Muir enrolled at the University of Wisconsin, but he quit before graduation to enter what he called "the University of the Wilderness." In 1867, after recovering from a factory accident that nearly left him blind, he embarked on a 1,000-mile walk to Florida.

From Florida Muir set sail for California, arriving in San Francisco in 1868. He immediately set out on a six-week walk to Yosemite. Spellbound by Yosemite's scenery—"every feature glowing, radiating beauty that pours into our flesh and bones like heat rays from fire"—Muir found employment the following summer as a sheepherder in the Sierra Nevada. Wandering the alpine meadows with a St. Bernard named Carlo, Muir rejoiced in the mountain wilderness. In his free time he studied plants and climbed tall peaks. "This June seems the greatest of all the months of my life," he wrote, "the most truly, divinely free." By the end of the summer, Muir had developed a passion for the Sierra Nevada, which he christened the "Range of Light."

The following summer Muir worked at a sawmill in Yosemite Valley, and for the next several years he rambled about the Sierra Nevada, meticulously studying the natural landscape and taking notes. He often wandered for days in the wilderness, carrying nothing more than a blanket, a notebook, some tea, and dry bread. Around this time Muir began writing popular nature articles for newspapers and magazines.

In 1880 Muir married the daughter of a wealthy California fruit farmer. Settling down for the first time in his life, he spent the next several years working the farm and raising two daughters. But domestic life wore on Muir, and in 1888 his wife sold par-

"Climb the mountains and get their good tidings. Nature's peace will flow through you as the sunshine into the trees. The winds will blow their freshness into you, and the storms their energy, while cares will drop off like autumn leaves."

cels of the family estate to allow Muir to focus on his wilderness studies. Shortly thereafter he teamed up with the influential editor Robert Underwood Johnston to spearhead the creation of Yosemite National Park.

In 1892 Muir co-founded the Sierra Club and became its first president. His first book, *The Mountains of California*, was published two years later when he was 56 years old. The book was an instant success, and several books followed that are now considered nature classics. "Strange is it not that a tramp and vagabond should meet such a fate," he wrote, "I never intended to write or lecture or seek fame in any way, I now write a great deal, and am well known." In 1903 Muir embarked on a year-long, round-the-world journey, then spent the final decade of his life fighting to stop the damming of Hetch Hetchy Valley in Yosemite. That battle was lost in 1913, and several months later Muir died of pneumonia.

Although Muir is often portrayed as a contemplative mountain poet, his younger days were characterized by brash, youthful machismo. His testosterone-fueled exploits included fleeing avalanches in winter, riding out storms in 100-foot trees, and generally risking life and limb. At one point he shimmied to the lip of Yosemite Falls just to check out the view. Such death-defying exploits profoundly influenced his writing. Whereas earlier environmental thinkers such as Emerson and Thoreau took leisurely strolls through the woods, Muir threw himself into nature with the physical vigor of an athlete.

Muir's eloquent, adventurous writing continues to resonate with audiences today. His ability to communicate the importance of wilderness preservation has influenced generations of prominent thinkers, and his once local celebrity has morphed into environmental superstardom. Today his likeness can be seen on T-shirts, posters and bumper stickers that read "Muir Power to You!"

Muir's sketch of the High Sierra

BECOMING A NATIONAL PARK

YOSEMITE VALLEY WAS officially protected in 1864, but under poor state management it developed into a cluttered series of roads, hotels, cabins and pastures for cattle. Land was tilled and irrigated to provide food for residents, and a timber mill provided wood for construction and heating.

Meanwhile, sheepherders grazed thousands of sheep in the pristine meadows high above Yosemite Valley. In 1870 Joseph LeConte remarked that "Tuolumne Meadows are celebrated for their fine pasturage. Some twelve to fifteen thousand sheep are now pastured here." The combined munching, chomping and trampling left the delicate meadows in disarray. During John Muir's first summer as a Sierra sheepherder, he witnessed this destruction firsthand. "To let sheep trample so divinely fine a place seems barbarous," he wrote. Later he put the destruction in even sharper terms, referring to sheep as "hooved locusts."

In 1889, after nearly a decade spent away from Yosemite, Muir returned with Robert Underwood Johnson, editor of the influential *Century Magazine*. Muir was shocked by what he saw. In the Mariposa Grove, a tunnel had been carved into a giant sequoia as a spectacle to draw tourists. In Yosemite Valley, trash littered the ground and once-pristine meadows had been converted to pasture. Distraught, the two men headed for the High Sierra.

Around a campfire in Tuolumne Meadows, Muir and Johnson discussed the beauty of Yosemite and the twin threats of development and grazing. Johnson suggested that Muir, who had become a well-known nature writer, become the public voice of a campaign to preserve Yosemite as a national park. Although Yosemite Valley and the Mariposa Grove were officially protected by the state (on paper, at least), Muir and Johnson believed the mountains surrounding Yosemite, and the watershed that fed Yosemite Valley, also deserved protection. Yellowstone had become America's first national park 17 years earlier, and the men believed Yosemite deserved similar status.

Returning from their camping trip, the two men embarked on a savvy media campaign to rally public support for their cause. Muir wrote two articles for *Century Magazine* extolling the beauty of Yosemite and the threats it faced. In his first piece, entitled "The Treasures of the Yosemite," Muir penned some of his most enduring prose. "No temple made with hands can compare with Yosemite," he wrote, "Every rock in its walls seems to glow with life ... as if into this one mountain mansion Nature had gathered her choicest treasures."

Muir and Johnson also stumped for the creation of Yosemite National Park in speeches around the country, and their tireless efforts were ultimately

Robert Underwood Johnson

Teddy Roosevelt & John Muir

rewarded. On October 1, 1890, Yosemite became America's third national park. To protect its nearly 1 million acres, units of the Army Cavalry were dispatched to Wawona. The cavalry patrolled the mountains on horseback, driving out sheepherders, cattlemen and hunters.

Despite the creation of Yosemite National Park, the original Yosemite Grant, which included Yosemite Valley and the Mariposa Grove, remained under California's protection. But California was not up to the task. In 1895 Muir described Yosemite Valley as "downtrodden, frowsy, and like an abandoned backwoods pasture. It looks ten times worse now than ... seven years ago. Most of the level meadow floor of the Valley is fenced with barbed and unbarbed wire and about three hundred head of horses are turned loose every night to feed and trample the flora out of existence ... As long as the management is in the hands of eight politicians appointed by the ever-changing Governor of California, there is but little hope."

Muir believed Yosemite Valley and the Mariposa Grove needed to be incorporated into Yosemite National Park to be truly protected. That was far easier said than done. Hotel owners in Yosemite Valley vigorously opposed the idea, fearing their businesses would be shut down if the Yosemite Grant was transferred to the federal government.

Salvation came in the form of President Theodore Roosevelt, who visited Yosemite in 1903. Although Roosevelt specifically requested that no fanfare or celebrations herald his arrival, local residents planned a lavish banquet attended by the governor of California and followed by an expensive fireworks display. Dismayed, Roosevelt asked Muir to show him the *real* Yosemite, and the two men quietly slipped into the backcountry for several nights of camping.

Around a roaring campfire, Roosevelt and Muir talked late into the night, slept in the brisk open air, and woke up to a dusting of snow. "I've had the time of my life," Roosevelt later told reporters. "Just think of where I was last night. Up there amid the pines and the silver firs, in the Sierran solitude, and without a tent. I passed one of the most pleasant nights of my life."

With President Roosevelt's support firmly in place, Muir and the Sierra Club lobbied to transfer the Yosemite Grant to the National Park Service. After a bitter fight in the California legislature, a bill was passed and sent to Washington. Again Muir stepped into action, cajoling Congressmen and pulling strings to secure the necessary votes. Finally, on June 11, 1906, President Roosevelt signed the bill into law.

Elated, Muir wrote to his old friend Johnson: "Sound the loud trimble and let every Yosemite tree and stream rejoice ... The fight you planned by that famous Tuolumne camp-fire seventeen years ago is at last fairly, gloriously won, every enemy down."

But unbeknownst to Muir, a new battle was looming on the horizon.

THE BATTLE FOR HETCH HETCHY

SIX WEEKS BEFORE Yosemite Valley officially became part of Yosemite National Park, San Francisco lay in ruins. On April 18, 1906, a massive earthquake shook the city, demolishing buildings and other man-made structures. Most of the damage occurred after the earthquake, when a massive fire raced through town and incinerated over 500 city blocks. With limited access to water, residents could do little but watch their glorious city burn. In the end, more than half of the city's 400,000 citizens were left homeless and roughly 3,000 people died. A century later, it remains the largest loss of life due to a natural disaster in California's history.

In spite of the catastrophe, the human spirit prevailed and the citizens of San Francisco rallied to rebuild their home. It was a remarkable effort, but a vexing problem remained: San Francisco, which is situated at the tip of a small peninsula, has no natural water supply.

During the boom years of the Gold Rush, fresh water was ferried to San Francisco on schooners, poured into large casks, and hauled up the city's steep streets by weary horses and mules. (Such sorry sights inspired Andrew Hallidie, an animal lover, to invent the cable car.) Later a Roman-style aqueduct—the first in America—delivered water from a large creek 20 miles distant.

By 1906, however, this limited water supply was completely inadequate for the city's booming population—a fact that became painfully clear in the wake of the earthquake. As civic leaders struggled to build a new and improved San Francisco, one of their top priorities was securing a large, reliable source of water. And one of the most promising sites for a new reservoir was Hetch Hetchy Valley in Yosemite National Park.

Lying just 25 miles north of Yosemite Valley, Hetch Hetchy was considered by many to be Yosemite's sister valley. It too was surrounded by massive granite cliffs and thundering waterfalls, and though smaller it was similarly beautiful. The famous geologist Josiah Whitney described Hetch Hetchy as "almost an exact counterpart of the Yosemite Valley [although] not on quite as grand a scale as that valley. But if there were no Yosemite, the Hetch Hetchy would be fairly entitled to a worldwide fame."

In 1871 John Muir called Hetch Hetchy "one of Nature's rarest and most precious mountain temples." When talk of a potential dam in Hetch Hetchy surfaced, Muir readied himself for battle. Other rivers could quench San Francisco's thirst, and Muir was determined to protect the beautiful valley where he had spent many happy days and nights. It was illegal, he pointed out, to build a dam in a national park. Dam proponents responded by introducing legislation to remove that technicality. When the legal sleight-of-hand was blocked, dam proponents presented the conflict as the thirsty citizens of San Francisco against a few wealthy hiking enthusiasts from the Sierra Club.

Following the earthquake, Muir was up against even longer odds. The emotionally and financially shattered residents of San Francisco were desperate for peace of mind, and feasibility studies indicated that Hetch Hetchy was the most cost-effective water source for the devastated city. Again the cry went up to dam Hetch Hetchy, but Muir and the Sierra Club fought back.

Insults were hurled back and forth, and the local battle soon spilled over into the national arena. One of the most prominent supporters of the dam was Gifford Pinchot, the brilliant young head of the U.S. Forest Service who preached conservation over preservation—so-called "wise use" that sought to sustainably protect natural resources while utilizing them for the greatest possible good. His argument for the dam at Hetch Hetchy struck a similar chord. "The injury," he wrote, "by substituting a lake for the present swampy floor of the valley ... is altogether unimportant compared with the benefits to be derived from its use as a reservoir." Visitation numbers seemed to support this—fewer than 300 people visited the swampy, mosquito-infested valley each summer.

Both Muir and Pinchot were devout proponents of wilderness protection, but their ideologies shared little else in common. Pinchot believed wild resources, used sustainably, should be put to the greatest possible good. Muir, ever the romantic, wanted strict preservation for recreational use only. "Dam Hetch Hetchy! As well dam for water-tanks the people's cathedrals and churches," wrote Muir, "for no holier temple has ever been consecrated by the heart of man." It was classic Muir, wrapping nature preservation in condemnatory, religious rhetoric. In a lighter moment Muir confided to a friend, "How this business Hetch-hetchs one's time. It won't even let me sleep."

As the two sides traded barbs, the fight dragged on for many years. Using his considerable influence, Muir enlisted support from many powerful friends, including Presidents Roosevelt and Taft, who blocked any legislation favoring the dam. When Woodrow Wilson became President in 1912, however, he sided with proponents of the dam.

In less than a year, the Raker Act, which authorized the damming of Hetch Hetchy, passed both houses of Congress and was signed into law. John Raker, the bill's main proponent, claimed the reservoir would be the "highest form of conservation," making the valley more accessible and useful for recreation. "As to damning the dammers they are damned already and buried beneath a roaring flood of lies," wrote Muir, who died a year later at the age of 76.

The battle over Hetch Hetchy was a milestone in American politics. It was the first national debate to pit economic growth against environmental preservation. As such, it set the tone for many future battles. The lessons learned by both sides were analyzed, critiqued and refined to a high art. In the 1950s, dam builders flooded scenic Glen Canyon in southern Utah. A few years later, the Sierra Club blocked two proposed dams in Grand Canyon using a brilliant PR campaign that paraphrased John Muir. Even today, the debate over wise-use versus strict preservation continues to rage.

Hetch Hetchy, pre-dam

"As in Yosemite, the sublime rocks of its walls seem to glow with life, whether leaning back in repose or standing erect in thoughtful attitudes, giving welcome to storms and calms alike, their brows in the sky, their feet set in groves and gay flowers, while birds, bees, and butterflies help the river and waterfalls to stir all the air into music—things frail and fleeting and types of permanence meeting here and blending, just as they do in Yosemite, to draw her lovers into close and confiding communion"

THE NATIONAL PARK SERVICE

THROUGHOUT THE HETCH HETCHY debate, the U.S. Cavalry dutifully looked after Yosemite. Although several national parks had been established by the turn of the century, the National Park Service had not yet been established, so the guardianship of Yosemite's fell to the military. After decades of exemplary service, the cavalry was replaced by a civilian force in 1914.

That same year, a wealthy industrialist named Stephen Mather wrote a letter of complaint to Secretary of the Interior Franklin K. Lane. Mather, who made his fortune mining borax in Death Valley, was frustrated with the way America's national parks were managed, and he demanded that something be done. Lane's response: "If you don't like the way the national parks are being run, come on down to Washington and run them yourself." Mather did just that, and for the next 14 years he shaped a strong vision for America's national parks.

Mather's first step was to establish a government agency to oversee the national parks. On August 25, 1916, President Woodrow Wilson signed the Organic Act, which established the National Park Service. Mather was named director of the new agency, and his first priority was to boost park visitation. More visitors meant more public support, which the fledgling agency desperately needed to justify its existence and ensure its survival.

To accommodate automobiles, which were becoming increasingly popular in Yosemite, Mather secured funds to replace roads designed for horses with roads designed for cars. The result was predictable: visitation boomed. In 1915 roughly 15,000 people visited Yosemite. Five years later, that number jumped to nearly 69,000 people.

To accommodate the new visitors, Mather championed the construction of new hotels. "Scenery," wrote Mather, "is a hollow enjoyment to a tourist who sets out in the morning after an indigestible breakfast and a fitful sleep on an impossible bed." The park soon offered a wide range of lodging options, but the crown jewel was the sumptuous Ahwahnee Hotel—an architectural masterpiece for Mather's favorite national park.

Despite the physical improvements, many basic problems remained. Yosemite was still riddled with inholdings (privately owned parcels of land purchased before the creation of the park) that were vulnerable to mining, logging and development. In 1930 John D. Rockefeller, Jr. put up half the money needed to purchase 15,000 acres of private land; the rest was provided by Congress.

Under Mather's watchful eye, Yosemite Valley became a recreational wonderland luring thousands of tourists each year. Decades later, with annual visitation well into the millions, some would question the wisdom of this policy. At the time, however, Mather's policies were essential to ensure the long-term survival of the National Park Service.

ANSEL ADAMS

Yosemite has inspired many artists, but none have become as singularly identified with the park as Ansel Adams. His stunning black and white photos elevated landscape photography to lofty new heights, and his dramatic visions of Yosemite still resonate with viewers around the world.

Born to an upper-class San Francisco family, Adams was an odd, hyperactive child. A talented musician, he dreamed of becoming a concert pianist, but while recovering from an illness he discovered a copy of James Hutchings' book *In the Heart of the Sierras*. Captivated by the photographs, Adams begged his family to visit Yosemite. In 1916 his dream came true, and upon entering Yosemite Valley Ansel's father presented him with a fateful gift: a small Kodak camera.

At 17 Adams joined the Sierra Club and participated in many High Sierra camping trips. He soon became frustrated with his simple camera, however, which took drab pictures that failed to convey the powerful emotions he felt. To remedy the situation, Adams immersed himself in advanced photography.

Over the next two decades, Adams produced hundreds of dazzling photographs distinguished by bold, lush tonality. Assorted darkroom techniques allowed him to heighten the drama, infusing wilderness scenes with personal emotion—what he *felt* in addition to what he saw. "When I'm ready to make a photograph," he said, "I see in my mind's eye something that is not literally there ... I'm interested in expressing something which is built up from within, rather than extracted from without."

Adams' rigorous work ethic and finely tuned creative instincts catapulted him to the top of the art world. Although his best work was done in his 20s and 30s—sometimes working at an unsustainable manic pace—in later life Adams eagerly adopted the role of elder statesmen. He campaigned on behalf of the American wilderness and endeared himself to the public with his enthusiasm and charm. Unlike many landscape photographers, Adams was a gregarious bon vivant. He relished parties, frequently holding forth at the piano while strong drinks were poured late into the night.

Adams served on the board of the Sierra Club for 37 years, and his gorgeous photographs inspired millions of Americans to embrace the outdoors. In 1940 his photographs of Kings Canyon helped convince Congress to turn it into a national park. Forty years later he was awarded the Presidential Medal of Freedom. Following his death in 1984, both the Ansel Adams Wilderness and Mount Ansel Adams in Yosemite were named in his honor.

Mount Ansel Adams

YOSEMITE ROCK STARS

BY THE DAWN of the 20th century, most famous peaks in Yosemite had been summited. A few first ascents were made by the California Geological Survey, which mapped the entire Sierra Nevada in the 1860s, but the Survey labeled many rugged peaks "inaccessible." Predictably, such declarations only whetted the appetites of adventurers, and soon every notable peak in Yosemite had been conquered.

In 1931, Harvard professor Robert Underhill visited the Sierra Nevada and introduced mountaineering techniques he learned in Europe. The Europeans had pioneered mountain climbing in the 1800s, and for decades they were the sport's preeminent practitioners. After Underhill's visit, Sierra Nevada alpinists began blazing difficult new routes up previously conquered peaks.

Following World War II and the invention of nylon rope, the sport of rock climbing forever changed. Prior to nylon, climbers used hemp ropes that snapped under sudden, intense pressure—a taut rope caused by a falling climber, for example. As a result, falling was a fatal mistake to be avoided at all costs. But the new, virtually unbreakable nylon ropes completely altered that equation. Adventurous climbers began attempting risky new moves that often caused them to fall. In the brave new post-nylon world, this was suddenly OK. Through dedicated trial and error, climbers perfected complex gravity-defying moves, and before long they were scampering up sheer vertical cliffs where no rational human belonged.

Armed with impressive new skills, climbers sought out bigger and bigger walls. And no place on Earth offered more fantastically big walls in a more gloriously accessible location than Yosemite. In the 1940s and '50s, a motley collection of climbers descended on the park to put their skills to the test. Among the new arrivals was a 47-year-old Swiss ironworker named John Salathé, who pioneered an important new piece of climbing equipment: the steel piton. This strong metal spike, fashioned with an eye-hole at one end, could be hammered into cracks to provide a safe, secure anchor for ropes.

Pitons already existed in Europe, but they were made with soft, malleable iron that often buckled in Yosemite's hard granite cracks. Salathé's steel pitons, by contrast, held strong. They could also be reused, which meant carrying less equipment on big climbs. Armed with steel pitons, Salathé unleashed another radical innovation in Yosemite: the multi-day climb. After climbing all day, Salathé spent the night strapped to the face of the rock. No longer constrained by equipment or daylight, climbers could rise as high as their bodies would take them.

Yosemite's pioneering "granite astronauts" soon conquered Yosemite Valley's most storied landmarks. Salathé kicked off the trend with the first multi-day ascent of Lost Arrow Spire (1947) and 1,500-foot Sentinel Rock (1950). In 1957 Royal Robbins, Jerry Gallwas, and Mike Sherrick climbed the vertical 2,000-foot Northwest Face of Half Dome in five days. The trio was graciously greeted at the

Lost Arrow Spire

top by Warren Harding, Robbins' chief rival. But following Robbins' achievement, Harding made it his personal mission to bag the biggest wall of all: El Capitan. In 1958 Harding and two friends, Wayne Merry and George Whitmore, attempted to reach the top of El Capitan using "siege tactics"—setting ropes higher and higher and rappelling down for rest and supplies. After 45 days spread over 18 months, the trio finally made it to the top. Robbins considered such tactics poor form, and in 1960 he assembled a group and retraced Harding's route in a single, committed seven-day push.

Over the next decade, many future climbing legends came to Yosemite Valley and left their mark, establishing dozens of challenging new routes. By the early 1970s, however, the popularity of rock climbing was exploding, and the once-minimal damage caused by pitons began to raise concerns. Hammering pitons into and out of cracks distorted the rock, leaving a rounded scar behind. Many popular routes were riddled with piton marks, and the damage was compounding each year.

In 1973 Galen Rowell, Dennis Henneck, and Doug Robinson climbed the Northwest Face of Half Dome using radical "clean" gear that left no trace. Rather than hammering in pitons, they wedged bolt-sized pieces of aluminum into hairline cracks. The aluminum pieces were fashioned in a wide variety of shapes and sizes to accommodate whatever cracks they encountered. Most importantly, they could be easily un-wedged without leaving a scar. *National Geographic* devoted a cover story to their endeavor, and chocks and nuts (as the metal pieces came to be called) soon became commercially available. A new era of rock conservation had begun. Any half-decent climber could hammer their way to the top of a route. But the new climbing philosophers believed it was better to rise to meet the challenge of the rock than to lower the difficulty of the climb to compensate for personal weakness.

In the 1980s, however, American climbers at other popular destinations began drilling small permanent bolts into rock faces to standardize climbs. This allowed climbers to focus less on equipment and more on pure athletic ability. Although bolts were often spaced widely apart to retain the challenge of the rock, this new style of climbing, called sport climbing, met with vehement resistance in Yosemite. Purists deplored the "excessive" bolt-drilling, and many verbal—and sometimes physical—confrontations ensued. "Sport Climbing Is Neither" mocked a popular bumper sticker. Gradually, however, the practice was grudgingly accepted, and an uneasy truce has remained in place ever since.

Today roughly five percent of Yosemite visitors—over 200,000 people—identify themselves as rock climbers. Young climbers come to follow in the footsteps of living legends, while old-timers climb well into their 60s, 70s, and even 80s. Today, as always, Yosemite Valley lies at the heart of American rock climbing. Its history, legends, and personalities have influenced generations of climbers, and they will continue to shape the sport in the years to come.

YOSEMITE TODAY

TODAY YOSEMITE IS one of America's most popular national parks, luring millions of visitors from around the globe. But the park's immense popularity poses significant challenges. In 1855, 42 people visited Yosemite Valley. A century later, annual visitation topped one million—and the numbers kept climbing. Two million in 1967, three million in 1987, four million in 1994. In Yosemite Valley, where most visitation is concentrated, peak-season traffic jams and long lines became as much a part of the scenery as cliffs and waterfalls. To alleviate congestion, the park service established one-way roads, initiated a free shuttle service, and reduced the number of hotel rooms and campsites.

Managing a park as large and popular as Yosemite is a complex, difficult task. The National Park Service bears the burden of both protecting the natural resources and providing for the enjoyment of park visitors—two often conflicting goals. In 2000 a general management plan outlined five main priorities for Yosemite: reduce visual intrusion of administrative and commercial services, reduce crowding, reduce traffic congestion, allow natural processes to prevail, and promote visitor understanding through enhanced interpretive programming and educational facilities. Successfully achieving these goals is an ongoing challenge. But with a dedicated staff, a passionate public, and the support of terrific organizations like the Yosemite Conservancy, Yosemite's future looks bright.

YOSEMITE VALLEY

★ ★ ★ ★ ★

YOSEMITE VALLEY

THREE-THOUSAND-FOOT cliffs. Thundering waterfalls. Sparkling granite domes. Yosemite Valley is, without question, the most spectacular part of the park. Just seven miles long and less than one mile wide, it's home to six waterfalls over 1,000 feet tall surrounded by some of the world's most dramatic alpine scenery. Its physical geography and picture-perfect layout are almost beyond belief. As John Muir wrote, it's "as if into this one mountain mansion Nature had gathered her choicest treasures."

Everyone is enchanted the first time they visit Yosemite Valley. But the more you get to know it, the more enchanting it becomes. From exquisite seasonal spectacles—the natural Firefall in February, the spring "moonbow" of Yosemite Falls—to the sun's final rays lighting up Half Dome at the end of each day, it seems impossible Yosemite Valley could have been created by chance. But the whimsical forces of geology—an upwelling of magma here, an Ice Age there—somehow conspired to produce this natural wonder. Learn more about the story behind the scenery and Yosemite Valley becomes even more sublime.

There are countless ways to spend your time in Yosemite Valley. Looking for adventure? There are 12 miles of bicycle paths, 63 miles of hiking trails, float trips down the Merced River, and some of the world's best rock climbing. Want to relax and marvel at the scenery? Lounge along the banks of the Merced River or take a narrated tram tour. And everyone should enjoy at least one free ranger program, with topics ranging from natural history to photography.

Over three million people visit Yosemite Valley each year. This means big crowds during peak season from June through September. Long lines, traffic jams, and parking hassles are not uncommon during the busiest months. But no matter how crowded Yosemite Valley gets—and on popular summer weekends it can get *very* crowded—nothing can take away from the jaw-dropping scenery.

Even if you visit during peak season, there are still a few tricks to escape the crowds. Tip #1: Head to popular sights in early morning or late afternoon—you'll avoid the worst of the crowds and enjoy the best light. Tip #2: Go for a hike. Crowds thin out exponentially every foot you climb (hyper-popular Mist Trail notwithstanding). And the highly underrated Valley Loop Trail is surprisingly crowd-free between popular sites.

Yosemite Valley
BASICS

Getting Around Yosemite Valley

A 13-mile paved road circles Yosemite Valley. Although it's possible to drive your car from sight to sight, parking is a minor hassle in spring and fall—and a *major* hassle in summer. My advice: park your car as soon as possible. Explore Yosemite Valley on foot, on bike, or on the free shuttle. Not only are these options easier, they're far more enjoyable.

Yosemite's free, year-round shuttle is a great way to explore eastern Yosemite Valley, which is filled with hotels, campgrounds, visitor facilities, and many popular sights. The shuttle also provide access to Happy Isles and Mirror Lake, which are closed to private vehicles. A seasonal summer shuttle heads as far west as El Capitan. The only downside: shuttles don't explore far west Yosemite Valley, which is home to great sights like Bridalveil Fall and Tunnel View. Check the *Yosemite Guide* for current shuttle routes and stops.

An even better way to explore Yosemite Valley is on foot or bike, traveling at your own pace and taking plenty of time to enjoy the scenery. Hikers can follow the 13-mile Valley Loop Trail, which circumnavigates the floor of Yosemite Valley. Bicyclists enjoy 12 miles of traffic-free bike paths adjacent to the main roads in eastern Yosemite Valley. Northside Drive and Southside Drive, which are also open to bicyclists, provide access to western Yosemite Valley.

Parking

There are two major parking areas in Yosemite Valley. The largest, the Village Day-Use Parking Area, is located just south of Yosemite Village. Another large parking area is located adjacent to Curry Village.

Visitor Centers and Info

The Valley Visitor Center in Yosemite Village (p.130) is the park's main visitor center. Information booths are also located in all Yosemite Valley hotels.

Lodging & Camping

There are four hotels and four campgrounds in Yosemite Valley (p.36).

Activities

RANGER PROGRAMS

Free ranger programs are one of the best ways to learn about Yosemite. Topics include natural history, human history, photography, and more. Evening campfire programs are also offered. Check the *Yosemite Guide* for seasonal schedules.

HIKING

See pages 166–184 for the best hikes in Yosemite Valley.

BIKING

Yosemite Valley has 12 miles of paved, car-free bike paths that showcase gorgeous scenery without the hassle of traffic and parking. Bike rentals are available at Curry Village and Yosemite Valley Lodge ($12/hour, $34/day).

RIVER RAFTING

In late spring/early summer you can float three easy miles down the Merced River, passing spectacular views of Yosemite Valley's cliffs and waterfalls. Four-person raft rentals are available at Curry Village ($30/person, including return shuttle).

TRAM & BUS TOURS

Bus tours and open-air tram tours depart daily from Yosemite Valley Lodge. There are guided tours of Yosemite Valley (including full moon tours), Glacier Point, and combo tours that include the Mariposa Grove of Giant Sequoias. Tickets ($38–110) are available at Yosemite Valley Lodge or travelyosemite.com.

YOSEMITE THEATER

From April to October, Yosemite Theater features nightly talks and performances. Topics range from pioneer history to modern-day search and rescue. The schedule is online at yosemite.org, and tickets available at Yosemite Valley Visitor Center.

ROCK CLIMBING

Yosemite Mountaineering School offers rock climbing classes for all levels from April through October. (209-372-8344, travelyosemite.com)

Groceries & Gear

VILLAGE STORE

The largest grocery store in Yosemite offers a good selection of meats, produce, condiments, snacks, firewood, beer, and wine. There's also an extensive selection of gifts and souvenirs.

YOSEMITE MOUNTAIN SHOP

Great selection of outdoor gear for hiking, camping, and rock climbing. Located next to the Curry Village Store. Open year-round. (209-372-8396)

Restaurants

★AHWAHNEE DINING ROOM $$$ (Brk, Lnch, Din)

Yosemite's top dining experience features delicious California cuisine served in the Ahwahnee Hotel's magnificent dining hall. Locally grown ingredients are prepared with French/Italian flair. The wine list features an extensive selection of California wines. Reservations are required for dinner and highly recommended for other meals. Attire is "Resort Casual" (which basically means no shorts). Open year-round (209-372-1489).

★THE MOUNTAIN ROOM $$$ (Din)

Yosemite Valley's other top-notch restaurant offers charcuterie, steaks, and sustainably harvested seafood. Good selection of California wines. The dining hall, located at Yosemite Valley Lodge, features impressive views of nearby Yosemite Falls. Open year-round (209-372-1274).

DEGNAN'S KITCHEN $$$ (Brk, Lnch, Din)

Your best bet for takeout in Yosemite Valley—perfect for a picnic lunch. Deli sandwiches, salads, soups, pizza, and baked goods. Located in Yosemite Village. Open year-round.

THE LOFT AT DEGNAN'S $$$ (Lnch, Din)

Upstairs from Degnan's Kitchen, Degnan's Loft serves BBQ, comfort food, beer, and wine in a pleasant, modern atmosphere. Open spring, summer, fall.

YOSEMITE LODGE FOOD COURT $$$ (Brk, Lnch, Din)

This cafeteria-style restaurant offers a bit of everything—soups, salads, pizza, burgers, pasta, and international fare. What it lacks in ambience it makes up for in selection. Located in Yosemite Valley Lodge. Open year-round.

CURRY VILLAGE PAVILION $$$ (Brk, Din)

The best food selection in Curry Village. Located near the amphitheater, Curry Village Pavilion serves cafeteria-style meals at moderate prices. The adjacent Coffee Corner serves coffee, cappuccino, espresso, and pastries. Open year-round.

PIZZA PATIO AT CURRY VILLAGE $$$ (Lnch, Din)

Hand-tossed pizzas and fresh salads. Enjoy your meal outdoors in the warmer months, or indoors when the temperature drops. Open year-round.

VILLAGE GRILL DECK $$$ (Brk, Lnch, Din)

Takeout burgers, fries, and other fast food. Located in Yosemite Village. Open spring, summer, fall.

MEADOW GRILL AT CURRY VILLAGE $$$ (Lnch, Din)

Takeout burgers, hot dogs, sandwiches, wraps, and salads. Open year-round.

Drinks & Cocktails

★AHWAHNEE BAR

Yosemite's most upscale bar, located in the sumptuous Ahwahnee Hotel, serves draft beer, wine, cocktails, and tasty appetizers. Enjoy a drink inside or soak in the dramatic views from the outdoor terrace. Open year-round.

★THE MOUNTAIN ROOM LOUNGE

Located at Yosemite Valley Lodge, the Mountain Room is Yosemite Valley's liveliest bar, luring a steady stream of rock climbers from nearby Camp 4 (p.136). Even if you don't climb (or drink), the Mountain Room's impressive collection of vintage Glen Denny rock climbing photos from the 1960s are worth a look. When the temperature drops, the fireplace is divine. Beer, wine, cocktails, and light appetizers available. Open year-round.

CURRY VILLAGE BAR

Located next to the Pizza Patio, Curry Village Bar serves draft beer and cocktails, which you can enjoy at the tiny bar or outside under the splendor of Yosemite Valley's tall cliffs. Open spring, summer, and fall.

Special Events

★BRACEBRIDGE DINNER

Half multi-course Christmas feast, half theater-in-the-round, Bracebridge Dinner is the Ahwahnee Hotel's most famous tradition. This Renaissance-style dinner, held every December since 1927, features a cast of over 100 richly costumed performers singing, dancing, and serving food. Based loosely on Washington Irving's classic account of an Old English feast, Bracebridge is popular, expensive, and worth it (bracebridgedinners.com, 801-559-5000).

★VINTNERS' HOLIDAYS

In November and December, the Ahwahnee Hotel hosts multi-day wine tastings, featuring rare and limited releases from California vineyards. Packages include hotel reservations, four wine-tasting sessions, a Meet the Vintners Reception, and a gourmet five-course meal (801-559-4884, travelyosemite.com).

CHEFS' HOLIDAYS

Held in January at the Ahwahnee Hotel, these multi-day packages combine fabulous accommodations with incredible food. Renowned chefs from California and beyond offer cooking demonstrations, a behind-the-scenes kitchen tour, a mix-and-mingle reception with the chef, and a five-course gala dinner with paired wines (801-559-4884, travelyosemite.com).

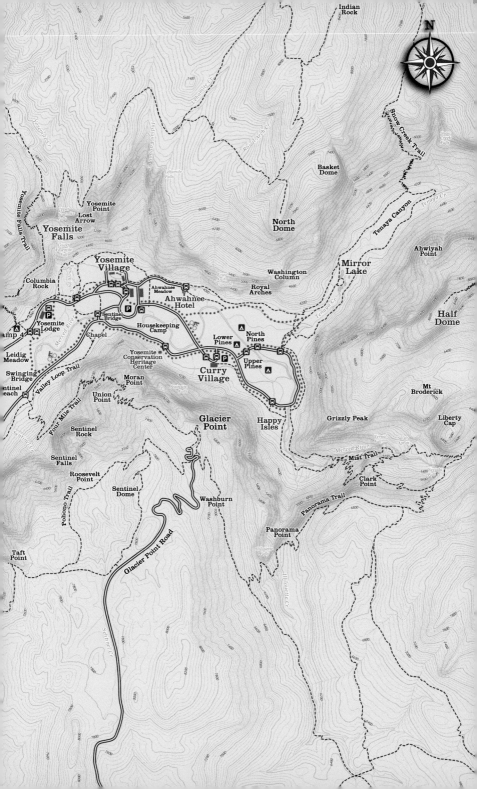

YOSEMITE VILLAGE

❶ YOSEMITE VALLEY VISITOR CENTER

The park's largest visitor center has a ranger-staffed help desk, the Yosemite Conservancy Bookstore, and a large exhibit hall exploring the history of Yosemite from geologic times to the present day. A short film, *Spirit of Yosemite*, plays free every half-hour. From April to October there are nightly performances at the Yosemite Theatre. Check the *Yosemite Guide* for current Yosemite Theatre offerings.

❷ YOSEMITE MUSEUM

This small, interesting museum displays beautiful baskets and artifacts from native tribes, plus exhibits on pioneer life in Yosemite Valley.

❸ INDIAN VILLAGE

An outdoor reconstruction of a traditional Ahwahneechee village, located behind the Yosemite Museum. The self-guided tour passes cedar-bark houses and native plant displays, offering a fascinating glimpse into the history of Yosemite Valley's native people.

❹ YOSEMITE CEMETERY

The final resting place of some of Yosemite Valley's most famous early residents, including James Hutchings (p.97) and Galen Clark (p.98), whose grave is surrounded by giant sequoias. A guide to the Yosemite Cemetery is available at the Visitor Center.

❺ ANSEL ADAMS GALLERY

This gallery/store features photographs, books, posters, and more from Yosemite's iconic photographer (p.113). Rotating exhibits also feature the work of contemporary artists. There's a good selection of camera supplies, plus free and paid photography classes.

❻ WILDERNESS CENTER

If you're planning on backpacking in Yosemite, you'll want to stop here to pick up wilderness permits (p.18) and inquire about current trail conditions. The Wilderness Center also offers a good selection of backpacking-specific books, plus bear canister rentals.

❼ POST OFFICE

Send Mom a postcard stamped "Yosemite National Park, CA 95389." Open Monday through Saturday.

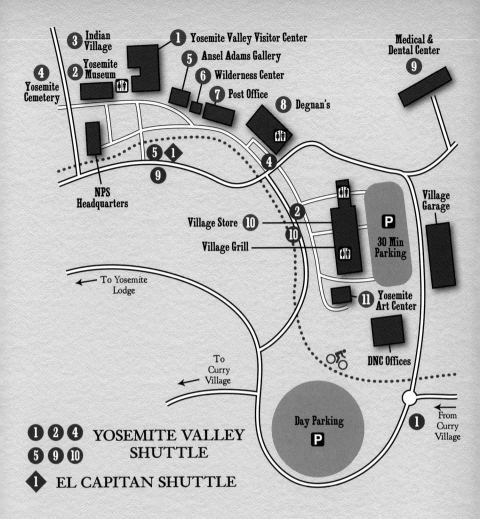

YOSEMITE VALLEY SHUTTLE ① ② ④ ⑤ ⑨ ⑩

EL CAPITAN SHUTTLE ◆①

⑧ DEGNAN'S KITCHEN & LOFT
Best takeout food in Yosemite Valley (p.126).

⑨ MEDICAL & DENTAL CENTER
Hopefully you won't end up here.

⑩ VILLAGE STORE
The largest store in Yosemite sells just about everything: fresh food, packaged food, beer, wine, T-shirts, books, and more.

⑪ YOSEMITE ART CENTER
The Yosemite Art Center offers mid-day art workshops Tuesday through Saturday during peak season. Check the *Yosemite Guide* for current offerings.

Yosemite Falls

This 2,425-foot, three-tiered waterfall is one of the park's most spectacular sights. If all three tiers are taken together, Yosemite Falls is the highest waterfall in North America and the fifth-highest waterfall in the world. (Venezuela's Angel Falls is the world's highest waterfall at 3,212 feet.) Yosemite Falls' three tiers consist of Upper Fall (1,430 feet), middle cascade (675 feet), and Lower Fall (320 feet). The Ahwahneechee call Yosemite Falls *Choo-Look* ("The Fall").

To see Yosemite Falls in full glory, timing is key. The waterfall drains roughly 40 square miles, and its flow depends almost entirely on snowmelt. Yosemite Falls generally peaks in May, when it can gush 100 cubic feet per second—enough to fill a large football stadium in less than a day. By mid-summer, however, the waterfall slows to a trickle, and by autumn it's completely dry. In winter, frozen mist and fallen ice form a 100- to 200-foot "snow cone" at the base of Upper Yosemite Falls. Another natural phenomenon, the rainbow-like "moonbow," appears in the mist during full moons in April and May.

Although there's a direct path to Lower Yosemite Falls from the Yosemite Falls Shuttle Stop (#6), it's better to follow the paved trail west (left) past the restrooms and picnic tables. This leads to a fabulous path that approaches Yosemite Falls head-on. As you walk down the path, all three tiers of Yosemite Falls are perfectly framed by towering pines.

Follow the path until you reach a three-dimensional bronze relief map of Yosemite Falls. Take a good look at the map and notice the hiking trail (p.184) that heads to the top of Yosemite Falls. Several hundred thousand years ago, Yosemite Falls tumbled down the upper reaches of this trail, which lies west of the waterfall's present course. Around 130,000 years ago, however, a melting glacier deposited a large pile of debris in the ancient streambed, which blocked the stream and diverted it along its present course.

Continue past the three-dimensional map until you can see the top of the waterfall through the trees. To the right of Yosemite Falls is Lost Arrow, a towering stone pinnacle that branches off the main cliff. The name Lost Arrow comes from an Ahwahneechee legend about a hunter celebrating a successful kill in the High Sierra. After the kill, the hunter shot an arrow in the air, and when it landed in Yosemite Valley the arrow turned to stone. Lost Arrow was the first "big wall" rock climb attempted in Yosemite Valley. In 1947 Anton Nelson and John Salathé spent five days climbing Lost Arrow—the first time in history anyone had spent more than a single night on a sheer rock face in Yosemite.

Continue uphill to the wooden bridge in front of Lower Yosemite Falls. In spring, when the waterfall is peaking, cool spray will soak your clothes. No matter when you visit, watch out below! The Ahwahneechee believe a group of evil spirit women called *Po'-loti* live in the waters below Yosemite Falls.

Yosemite Falls

Black Oaks

These beautiful trees provided the Ahwahneechee with their most important food: acorns. The black oaks of Yosemite Valley often yield several tons of acorns each autumn. A multi-day feast accompanied the annual harvest, but most acorns were stored for winter use. Acorns from black oaks were considered the tastiest in California, and the Ahwahneechee used acorn flour in soup, gruel, and bread.

Camp 4

At first glance this crowded cluster of tents seems like a campsite of last resort. But Camp 4 is one of rock climbing's holiest temples—a global mecca on par with Base Camp at Mount Everest. Its legacy began in the 1950s, when early rock climbers came to Yosemite to conquer the park's famous cliffs. Scraping out a meager existence in Camp 4, they spent years honing the culture and craft of modern rock climbing, pioneering techniques that ultimately spread around the world. By day these "granite astronauts" conquered Yosemite Valley's big walls. By night they discussed their exploits around roaring campfires. Over the years, as rock climbing grew in popularity, Camp 4 developed a reputation as Yosemite's Climber's Camp. One scraggly climber named Yvon Chounard sold homemade climbing equipment in the parking lot, a business that ultimately grew into the outdoor clothing company Patagonia.

In January 1997 a "Flood of the Century" washed out many of Yosemite Valley's low-lying buildings and campsites. In response, the National Park Service decided to permanently shut down Camp 4. Upon hearing the news, a group of climbers united to save the fabled campsite. The climbers met with park service officials and explained the unique role Camp 4 played in the history of rock climbing. Climbers from around the world flooded the National Park Service with letters and phone calls attesting to the global importance of the site. Suddenly aware of Camp 4's unique heritage, the National Park Service agreed to keep the campsite open, and in 2003 it was listed on the National Register of Historic Places.

Camp 4 has been called both "tent ghetto" and "home of the gods" by rock climbers—a fact that speaks volumes about the grungy, tribal nature of the sport. For many, Camp 4 is as much about socializing as rock climbing. It's where members of a scattered, global subculture go to meet, greet, see, and be seen. Friendships are made, gossip is swapped, rivalries are born, and life goes on pretty much as it always has since climbers made Camp 4 their unofficial home away from home.

Devils Elbow

Gloriously situated beneath El Capitan, this sandy bend in the Merced River is the perfect place to lounge and watch the hours drift by. Located about 1.5 miles past Camp 4, Devils Elbow is best in mid- to late summer when the water level of the Merced River is low. While relaxing on the banks of the river, take a look at the dark splotch on the eastern face of El Capitan. Because the splotch bears a faint resemblance to North America, this section of El Capitan is called the North American Wall.

Devils Elbow

The Ahwahneechee Legend of Tutokanula

Long ago, two bear cubs wandered away from their mother and fell asleep on a rock near the Merced River. As they slept, the rock rose high into the sky, and the cubs became stranded. All of the forest animals tried to climb the cliffs to rescue the cubs, but no one—not Fox, not Coyote, not Mountain Lion—could reach the top. Finally, a tiny inchworm called Tutoka offered his help. At first the other animals laughed, but Tutoka slowly made his way up the cliff. As the inchworm climbed, he chanted "Tu-tok ... Tu-tok ... Tu-tok-a-nu-la!" Upon reaching the top, Tutoka guided the two bear cubs down to safety.

El Capitan

This imposing granite monolith, which rises 3,593 feet above the floor of Yosemite Valley, is the world's largest chunk of exposed, unbroken granite. Considered the crown jewel of American rock climbing, it attracts thousands of climbers from around the globe. During peak climbing season in spring and fall, El Capitan's sheer cliffs are covered with dozens of rock climbers. All told, there are over 70 routes to the top. The pullout on the road in front of El Capitan is a great place to watch climbers. In spring and fall, climbing rangers offer daily Ask A Climber programs in El Capitan Meadow. At night, you can often see climbers' headlamps twinkling thousands of feet above.

It takes rock climbers an average of four to six days to reach the top of El Capitan. All food, water, and supplies must be hauled up the cliff. If a climber drinks one gallon of water per day, they must haul 50 pounds of water for a six-day climb. After climbing all day, climbers spend the night on portable platforms strapped to the face of the rock. In addition to the physical, technical, and mental challenges, all solid human waste must be collected and carried off the cliff. For years climbers brought along homemade "poop tubes" made from sawed-off sections of PVC pipe. Today special sanitary bags are the disposal method of choice.

The first climber to conquer El Captain was Warren Harding, who pioneered The Nose route with two friends in 1958. Using "siege tactics" (setting fixed ropes higher and higher and rappelling down for rest and supplies), it took the team 45 days spread over 18 months to reach the top. Royal Robbins, Harding's rival, considered such tactics poor form, and in 1960 he assembled a team that climbed The Nose in a self-contained, seven-day ascent. In 1975 Jim Bridwell led a team on the first one-day ascent of The Nose. And in 1993 female rock climber Lynn Hill became the first person to free-climb The Nose. (In free-climbing ropes and gear are used only for protection.) The following year Hill returned and free-climbed The Nose in a single day. In 2018, Alex Honnold and Tommy Caldwell set El Capitan's speed record when they scaled The Nose in a remarkable 1 hour, 58 minutes, and 7 seconds.

El Capitan's most astonishing climb, however, was Alex Honnold's daring 2017 free solo (climbing with no ropes or protection), chronicled in the Oscar-winning documentary *Free Solo*. Although Honnold survived, over two dozen rock climbers have died on El Capitan since 1958.

Many people dream about climbing *up* El Capitan, but a few people are obsessed with jumping off of it. The first successful BASE jump was in 1966, but multiple deaths led the park service to ban the sport in 1980. In 1999 a BASE jumper drowned in the Merced River while trying to elude park rangers after an illegal jump off El Capitan. In response, a group of BASE jumpers organized a "protest" jump to showcase the safety of the sport. As spectators watched from below, a 58-year-old woman jumped off the top of El Capitan. Her parachute failed to open, however, and she died upon impact.

The Nose

Freerider

Dawn Wall

El Capitan

Climbing El Capitan

El Capitan is the world's premier rock climbing destination, and there are over 70 named routes on the wall. The most popular is The Nose, which offers the shortest, most direct route to the top. The Nose was first climbed in 1958 over multiple days, but speed climbers now complete it in under three hours. In 2015 Tommy Caldwell and Kevin Jorgeson took 19 days to climb the smooth granite on Dawn Wall—considered the hardest, longest free climb in the world. Two years later, Adam Ondra completed Dawn Wall in under eight days. On June 3, 2017, Alex Honnold became the first human to climb El Capitan using no ropes or safety equipment at all, free soloing Freerider in under four hours. Three days later, Leah Pappajohn and Jonathan Fleury completed the first naked ascent of El Capitan on The Nose.

Climbers' lights on El Capitan at night

"The modicum of moonlight that fell into this awful gorge gave to that precipice a vagueness of outline, an indefinite vastness, a ghostly and weird spirituality. Had the mountain spoken to me in audible voice ... I should hardly have been surprised."

—Horace Greeley, 1859

Tunnel View

This glorious viewpoint is one of Yosemite's must-see destinations. Perched high above Yosemite Valley's western entrance, it reveals some of the park's most spectacular landmarks—Bridalveil Fall, El Capitan, Half Dome—marching across the horizon. The sweeping panorama was immortalized by Ansel Adams in his iconic 1935 photograph "Clearing Winter Storm," which depicts a desolate Yosemite Valley in the wake of a snowstorm. These days, however, Tunnel View is often jam-packed with dozens of selfie-snapping tourists. If you're looking for peace and quiet, follow the steep trail that starts from the smaller parking area across the road. The trail heads to Old Inspiration Point, a lesser-known viewpoint located along an old, abandoned wagon road. After hiking a few hundred yards up the trail, you'll be treated to views nearly as dramatic as Tunnel View—but with a fraction of the crowds.

Gazing across Yosemite Valley, the landscape seems eternal. But the present view is different from the one visitors enjoyed in the 1850s. Prior to the arrival of Europeans, Yosemite Valley had larger meadows and open forests with trees spaced widely apart—the result of small, regular fires set by the Ahwahneechee. Mature trees survived the small fires due to thick bark, but the fires cleared out unwanted vegetation such as saplings encroaching upon meadows and leaf litter on the forest floor. This created open spaces that made travel and hunting much easier. Such landscapes also favored the animals that the Ahwahneechee liked to hunt. Far from being untouched, Yosemite Valley was actively "gardened" by the Ahwahneechee. Throughout much of the 20th century, however, the National Park Service followed a policy of fire suppression to "preserve" Yosemite Valley, which inadvertently led to smaller meadows and overgrown forests. Today the park service sets intentional, small fires to help return Yosemite to a more natural state. (See p.64 for more about fire in Yosemite.)

"The grandeur of the scene was softened by the haze that hung over the valley—light as gossamer—and by the clouds which partially dimmed the higher cliffs and mountains. This obscurity of vision but increased the awe with which I beheld it, and as I looked, a peculiar exalted sensation seemed to fill my whole being, and I found my eyes in tears with emotion."

—Dr. Lafayette Bunnell, 1851

Bridalveil Fall

This elegant, 620-foot waterfall is one of Yosemite Valley's most popular sights. Gusts of wind often fan the waterfall's lower curtain, giving it the appearance of a white, lacy veil, which inspired early explorers to name it Bridalveil. The Ahwahneechee call the waterfall Pohono ("Spirit of the Puffing Wind"). Bridalveil Fall is most dramatic between April and June, when melting snow results in peak runoff. During this time, a late afternoon rainbow can be seen from the parking area. Near the base of the waterfall, reached by a quarter-mile path from the parking area, you can sometimes see a double rainbow.

Bridalveil Fall is a textbook example of a "hanging valley." Before the Ice Age, the Sierra Nevada Mountains were filled with steep V-shaped valleys carved by rivers over millions of years. One of these valleys, the Merced River Canyon, was the precursor to Yosemite Valley, and Bridalveil Creek cascaded down its steep V-shaped walls. During the Ice Age, however, glaciers flowed through Merced River Canyon and carved out a broad, U-shaped valley with vertical cliffs. When the glaciers melted, Bridalveil Creek tumbled over the edge of a cliff, leaving its previous river valley "hanging."

Bridalveil Fall drains about 20 square miles—roughly half the size of the watershed of Yosemite Falls. And yet Bridalveil Fall often flows well into autumn, long after Yosemite Falls dries up. What's going on? Although Bridalveil Fall drains a smaller watershed, its watershed was never scraped bare by glaciers, so its deep soil retains more moisture that helps prolong its flow.

Cathedral Spires

Cathedral Beach Picnic Area

This shady picnic area, nestled among ponderosa pines and incense cedars, offers great swimming in summer along a sandy section of the Merced River. To the south lies Cathedral Spires (left), a pair of rock pinnacles that rise 1,900 feet above the Valley floor. To the north you'll enjoy tremendous views of El Capitan's southwest face. Just east of El Capitan lies The Three Brothers (above), an unusual three-tiered rock formation formed by parallel faulting, which is a fancy way of saying the rock eroded along three diagonal cracks. In 1987 a massive rockfall sent 1.5 million tons of granite tumbling down from The Three Brothers, leveling trees and tossing giant boulders into the Merced River hundreds of yards away. The Ahwahneechee name for the humped rock formation was *Kom-po-pai-zes*, which early explorer Dr. Lafayette Bunnell recorded as "mountains playing leapfrog." But this was not the actual translation. Bunnell himself admitted that "a literal translation is not desirable." Had Bunnell been less inclined towards G-rated prose, he might have translated *Kom-po-pai-zes* as "people engaged in an act of passion."

Sentinel Beach Picnic Area

This picnic area is similar to Cathedral Beach Picnic Area, with picnic tables and a restroom nestled among a shady grove of trees. This is also the stopping point for Merced river rafters (p.125).

Sentinel Falls

This classic "stairstep" waterfall tumbles down a series of mini-waterfalls, which, if added together, measure 2,000 feet. This makes Sentinel Falls the second-highest waterfall in North America after Yosemite Falls. By volume, however, Sentinel Falls is rather small, so it normally flows only in spring and early summer. Although Sentinel Falls often dries up by mid-summer, towering Sentinel Rock stands guard to the left year-round. According to early California geologist Josiah Whitney, 7,038-foot Sentinel Rock was named for its "fancied likeness to a gigantic watch-tower."

Yosemite Chapel

Built in 1879, this tiny chapel is the oldest building in Yosemite Valley still in use today. Blessed with stunning views of Yosemite Falls and the surrounding cliffs, the chapel is popular for weddings, marriage vow renewals, baptisms, and other special occasions (yosemitevalleychapel.org). Non-denominational services are open to the public every Sunday at 9:15am. A second service is held at 11am from Labor Day through Memorial Day.

Sentinel Falls

Yosemite Conservation Heritage Center

This charming stone building is the Sierra Club's home away from home in Yosemite Valley. Inside you'll find exhibits chronicling the history of the Sierra Club and a terrific library filled with nature books. The building is open 10am to 4pm, May through September. Free nature programs are often offered.

The building was constructed in 1903 in honor of Dr. Joseph LeConte, a geologist known for his eloquent nature writing and one of the first professors at the University of California, Berkeley. In *A Journal of Ramblings Through the High Sierras of California* LeConte wrote, "Was there ever so venerable, majestic, and eloquent a minister of natural religion as the grand old Half Dome?" LeConte was good friends with John Muir, and the two men became founding members of the Sierra Club in 1892.

LeConte died of a heart attack in Yosemite Valley in 1901. Shortly thereafter, a group of friends, professors, and former students donated money to construct a building in his honor. LeConte Memorial Lodge was originally built in Curry Village, but the building was moved to its present location in 1912. From the front porch you can enjoy lovely views of Half Dome and Yosemite Falls. For several years the building served as Yosemite Valley's main visitor center, and between 1920 and 1923 Ansel Adams served as its caretaker. In 2016 the Sierra Club changed the name of LeConte Memorial Lodge because LeConte, a former Georgia slave owner, wrote books and articles about the post-Civil War South that included derogatory racial passages.

Curry Village

Located 3,000 feet below Glacier Point, Curry Village is one of Yosemite Valley's main visitor hubs. This dense cluster of tent cabins, wood cabins, shower houses, shops, and restaurants throbs with activity in spring, summer, and fall.

Curry Village was established in 1899 by David and Jennie Curry. Although other hotels already existed in Yosemite Valley, at two dollars per night "Camp Curry" undercut them by half. Its motto was "Three squares a day, a clean napkin every meal, and NO tipping!" Each morning at sunrise David Curry bellowed out, "Those who do not rise for breakfast by eight am will have to postpone it until tomorrow. At eight o'clock the cook gets *hot* and burns the breakfast!"

The Currys started with just seven tent cabins, but Camp Curry proved extremely popular. Within a few years there were hundreds of tent cabins, a dance pavilion, pool hall, and winter ice skating rink. (The ice skating rink still operates today.) To entertain guests after sundown, Camp Curry offered evening programs featuring music, singing, and storytelling. But the most famous attraction was the Firefall (see following page). Today the original "Camp Curry" sign still hangs over the entrance, evening programs still entertain visitors, and over 400 tent cabins continue to offer Yosemite Valley's best budget lodging.

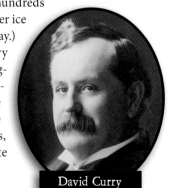

David Curry

Horsetail Falls

The Firefall

For nearly 100 years, from 1872 to 1968, the Firefall was one of Yosemite Valley's most popular sights. Every summer night, park employees pushed a huge pile of red-hot embers off the edge of Glacier Point, creating a glittering "waterfall" of fire that tumbled down 3,000 feet. The spectacle drew thousands of visitors to Curry Village, where the views were most spectacular. At 9pm sharp, a master of ceremonies shouted "Let The Fire Fall!" and the embers tumbled down as live music played.

In 1968 the park service permanently ended the Firefall, which by that point was considered artificial and unnatural. But a few years after the Glacier Point Firefall was extinguished, a "natural Firefall" was discovered on the opposite side of Yosemite Valley. During the last two weeks of February, weather permitting, the sun's final rays stream through Yosemite Valley at just the right angle and light up Horsetail Fall, which tumbles down the eastern face of El Capitan. Today the natural Firefall attracts photographers and spectators from around the world. Hotels are booked months in advance, and photographers arrive hours before sunset to stake out the perfect spot. For more on the Firefall, visit yosemitefirefall.com.

Half Dome

This extraordinary peak looms over the eastern end of Yosemite Valley like a granite monarch. Rising over 4,800 feet above the Valley floor, Half Dome reaches a maximum height of 8,842 feet. From most viewpoints in Yosemite Valley, Half Dome's rounded backside and sheer eastern face look like half of a giant granite dome. But this is an optical illusion. Viewed from Washburn Point (p.193), Half Dome's rounded backside is nearly as steep as its sheer northwest face. Take a look at the three dimensional map of Yosemite Valley at the Yosemite Valley Visitor Center (p.130)) and you'll see that Half Dome is actually a narrow, elongated ridge. Some geologists estimate that roughly 80 percent of the original "dome" is still intact. If you've ever wondered what happened to the other half of Half Dome, the unsatisfying answer is: there never was another half!

So what accounts for Half Dome's sheer, 2,200-foot northwest face? When Half Dome formed millions of years ago (due to compressional forces and the erosion of overlying rocks), it was riddled with vertical cracks. During the Ice Age, when glaciers repeatedly flowed down Tenaya Canyon, they chipped off rocks along vertical cracks in Half Dome's northwest face. But geologists believe that the upper 500 to 900 feet of Half Dome protruded above even the highest glaciers. The upper cliffs on Half Dome's northwest face were likely shaped by rockfalls along vertical cracks, which were accelerated by the glacial removal of the supporting rocks below.

In 1868 California state geologist Josiah Whitney proclaimed that Half Dome was "probably the only one of all the prominent points about the Yosemite which never has been, and never will be, trodden by human foot." Not surprisingly, attempts to climb it were soon underway. Although any decent hiker can easily reach the rounded backside of Half Dome, the final 700-foot, 45-degree ascent is too steep to hike.

In 1875 Yosemite Valley blacksmith George Anderson attempted to climb Half Dome's backside by applying sticky pine pitch to the bottom of his bare feet. When that didn't work, he spent several weeks drilling iron eye-bolts into the granite, then strung the bolts together with rope to reach the 13-acre summit. Anderson's rope-strung bolts remained the standard route for years, but they were later replaced with a slightly more advanced metal cable system. Today thousands of hikers trek to the top of Half Dome each year. (See page 174 to learn more about hiking Half Dome.)

In the 1950s, ambitious rock climbers set their sights on Half Dome's sheer northwest face. In 1957 Royal Robbins successfully led a team of rock climbers on the first ascent of Half Dome's northwest face. The astounding five-day climb was considered the hardest route in North America at the time. Ten years later Liz Robbins, Royal's wife, became the first woman to climb the northwest face of Half Dome.

The Ahwahneechee Legend of Tissayak

Long ago, a woman named Tissayak and her husband Nangas traveled to Yosemite Valley from the arid plains. Exhausted after the long journey, Nangas lost his temper and hit Tissayak. As Tissayak ran up Yosemite Valley, acorns spilled out of her basket, and those acorns grew into oak trees. When Tissayak reached Mirror Lake she drank it dry, and when thirsty Nangas arrived he grew enraged and hit her again. As Tissayak threw her basket at Nangas, the angry gods turned the couple into stone. Nangas became North Dome (with Basket Dome above) and Tissayak became Half Dome, her tears marked by dark streaks on the vertical face. And so, for the rest of eternity, the quarreling couple must face each other in silence.

Happy Isles

Named for three small islands in the Merced River, Happy Isles is the jumping-off point for Yosemite's most popular hike: the Mist Trail (p.168), which also heads to Nevada Fall (p.168) and Half Dome (p.174). Because the road to Happy Isles is off limits to private vehicles, visitors must walk here or take the free shuttle. A short distance from shuttle stop #16 is the family-friendly Nature Center at Happy Isles (open May–mid-Sept). This small museum is filled with natural history displays and serves as Yosemite's headquarters for the Junior Ranger Program. During peak season you can purchase snacks at the kiosk near the Happy Isles Shuttle Stop.

In July 1996, Happy Isles was the site of one of Yosemite Valley's most devastating rockfalls. Over 70,000 tons of rock detached from the cliffs above and went into free fall. A few seconds later, the rocks hit the ground at roughly 260 mph. The impact generated a 250 mph blast of wind that toppled more than 700 trees and sent rock fragments hurtling through the air. Remarkably, only one hiker was killed. Even today, you can still see many fallen trees in the vicinity of Happy Isles.

Mirror Lake

Mirror Lake is a great destination for anyone looking to escape the crowds and soak in Yosemite's natural scenery. A paved, one-mile trail starts at shuttle stop #17, crosses Tenaya Creek Bridge, and heads up a slight grade to Mirror Lake. From there an easy, unpaved 5-mile loop circumnavigates the lake. The reflections that give Mirror Lake its name are best viewed in spring and early summer, when the water level is highest. For the best reflections, walk along the east side of the lake in the morning or the west side of the lake in the late afternoon.

These days Mirror Lake is more of a pond than a lake—and it grows smaller each year. As more and more silt and vegetation accumulates, the lake is slowly filling in. Someday in the not-so-distant future, Mirror Lake will become Mirror Meadow. Mirror Lake originally formed following the largest known rockfall in Yosemite Valley, when over 15 million cubic yards of rocks crashed down from the cliffs above. The rockfall dammed Tenaya Creek and created Mirror Lake. The path to Mirror Lake from the shuttle stop actually travels over the rocky dam created by the enormous rock avalanche.

In March 2009, a much smaller rockfall originating at Ahwiyah Point sent roughly 45,000 cubic meters of rock tumbling below Half Dome. The resulting air blast knocked down over 100 trees, and the crash was equivalent to a 2.4 earthquake as measured by nearby seismometers. The rockfall buried a southern section of the Mirror Lake trail, closing it for over three years until workers established a new path.

Mirror Lake

Ahwahnee Hotel

The Ahwahnee Hotel is the pinnacle of luxury in Yosemite Valley. Its most expensive suite, which comes with it own library parlor, rents for over $1,000 per night. But even non-guests can enjoy a stroll through the hotel's sumptuous interior or a meal in the grand dining room (p.126). And nothing tops off a long day of hiking like a cold drink at the lovely hotel bar. Guided tours of the hotel are offered throughout the year (inquire at the concierge desk).

The Ahwahnee Hotel opened in 1927. Its construction was spearheaded by Stephen Mather, the first director of the National Park Service, who wanted a world-class lodge for his favorite national park. From a distance the hotel appears to be constructed of stone and timber, but a closer look reveals that the "timber" is actually molded concrete. In the early 1900s fire destroyed several grand lodges in other national parks, so Mather insisted that the Ahwahnee be fire-resistant. Although concrete supports were used, they were poured into wood-grain molds and painted to look like wood. Real timber is found only in the dining room.

Dozens of celebrities have spent the night at the Ahwahnee Hotel, including Queen Elizabeth II, Eleanor Roosevelt, and presidents John F. Kennedy and Barack Obama (both of whom arrived by helicopter). Lucille Ball, Desi Arnaz, and Judy Garland stayed here while filming *The Long, Long Trailer*. So did William Shatner and Leonard Nimoy while filming *Star Trek IV*. Robert Redford worked at the Ahwahnee as a young man, and Steve Jobs was married on the back lawn in a Buddhist ceremony.

Ahwahnee Dining Room

The Ahwahnee's Great Lounge is famous for warm fires in winter and tea and cookies served daily at 4pm. If the room seems hauntingly familiar, there's a good reason: it was used as a model for one of the interior sets in Stanley Kubrick's 1980 film *The Shining*.

⇜ VALLEY LOOP TRAIL ⇝

SUMMARY The Valley Loop Trail offers a rare opportunity to experience the natural beauty of Yosemite Valley with minimal crowds. Yosemite's most underrated trail makes a 13-mile loop around Yosemite Valley, from Yosemite Village to Bridalveil Meadow. Along the way you'll pass many of Yosemite Valley's top sights. You won't avoid crowds at popular sights, but long stretches of the Valley Loop Trail in between are delightfully crowd-free. While others are desperately searching for parking or waiting in long lines for packed shuttles, you'll be strolling through Yosemite Valley as John Muir intended. You can start or stop the Valley Loop Trail at multiple points in Yosemite Valley, including Yosemite Falls, Camp 4, El Capitan Bridge, Sentinel Bridge, and a junction with the Four Mile Trail. One of the most popular sections is a 7.2-mile half loop that starts at Yosemite Falls and crosses the Merced River at El Capitan Bridge. Bike and foot paths in eastern Yosemite Valley link the Valley Loop Trail to Happy Isles, Mirror Lake, and the Ahwahnee Hotel.

TRAILHEAD There's no official start or finish to the Valley Loop Trail.

◆ **TRAIL INFO** ◆

DIFFICULTY: Moderate   **HIKING TIME:** 1–7 hours

DISTANCE: 13 miles   **ELEVATION CHANGE:** 100 feet

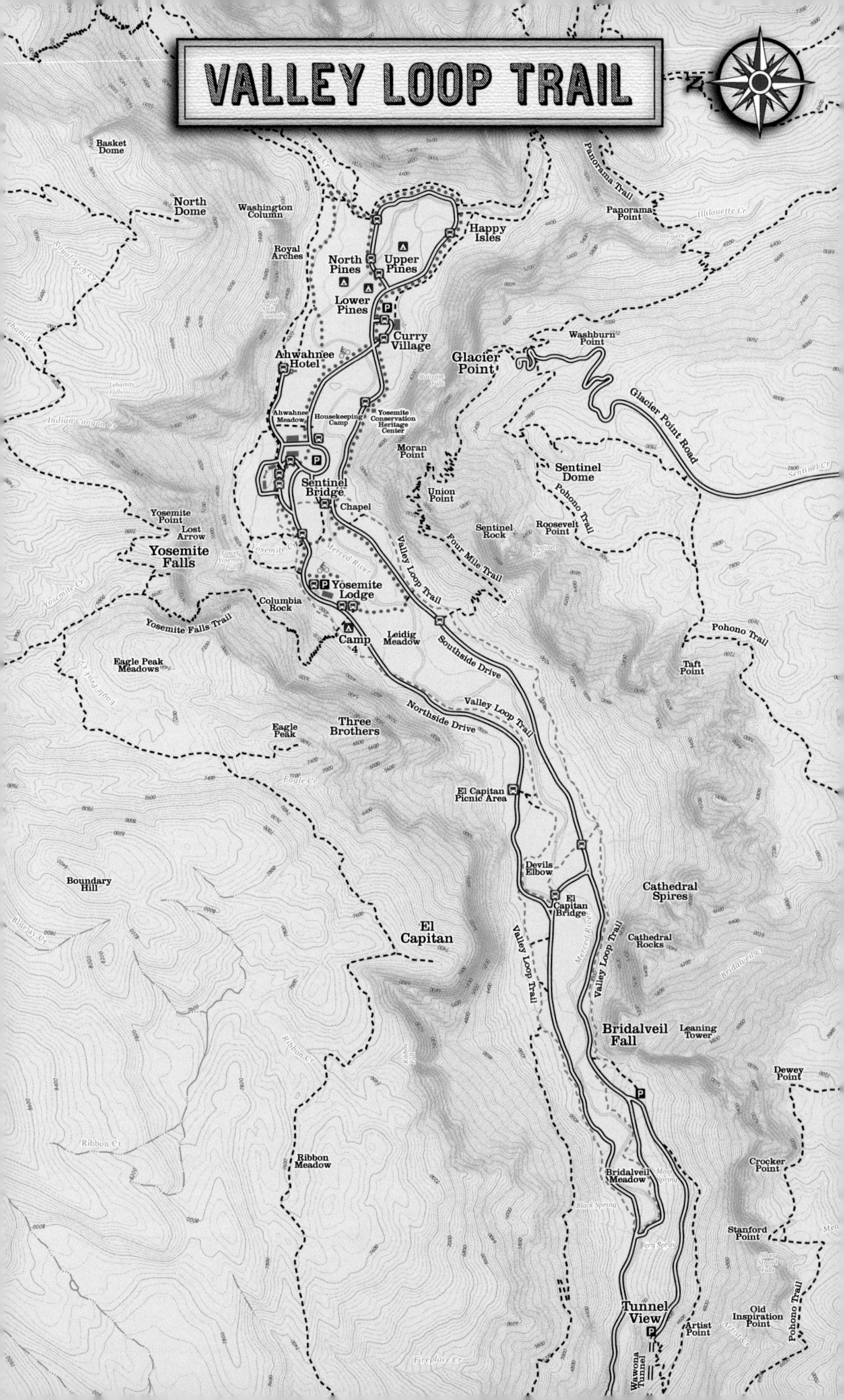
VALLEY LOOP TRAIL
N
Basket Dome
North Dome
Washington Column
Royal Arches
Royal Arch Cr
North Pines
Upper Pines
Lower Pines
Happy Isles
Curry Village
Panorama Trail
Panorama Point
Illilouette Cr
Washburn Point
Glacier Point
Glacier Point Road
Sentinel Cr
Ahwahnee Hotel
Ahwahnee Meadow
Housekeeping Camp
Yosemite Conservation Heritage Center
Moran Point
Indian Canyon Cr
Sentinel Dome
Pohono Trail
Sentinel Bridge
Chapel
Union Point
Sentinel Rock
Roosevelt Point
Yosemite Point
Lost Arrow
Yosemite Falls
Merced River
Four Mile Trail
Valley Loop Trail
Yosemite Lodge
Columbia Rock
Yosemite Cr
Yosemite Falls Trail
Camp 4
Leidig Meadow
Southside Drive
Pohono Trail
Taft Point
Eagle Peak Meadows
Eagle Peak Cr
Valley Loop Trail
Northside Drive
Eagle Peak
Three Brothers
Eagle Cr
El Capitan Picnic Area
Devils Elbow
El Capitan Bridge
Boundary Hill
Cathedral Spires
Cathedral Rocks
Bridalveil Cr
El Capitan
Valley Loop Trail
Valley Loop Trail
Bridalveil Fall
Leaning Tower
Ribbon Cr
Dewey Point
Ribbon Cr
Ribbon Meadow
Bridalveil Meadow
Crocker Point
Black Spring
Stanford Point
Fern Spring
Tunnel View
Old Inspiration Point
Artist Point
Pohono Trail
Wawona Tunnel
Fireplace Cr

❧ THE MIST TRAIL ℘

SUMMARY The Mist Trail is the most popular trail in Yosemite—and with good reason. Although relatively short by Yosemite standards, it passes some of the park's most dramatic scenery. The Mist Trail skirts the banks of the Merced River, crosses a bridge with great views of Vernal Fall, then heads up a series of stone steps in front of the 317-foot waterfall. In spring and early summer, the thundering waterfall soaks hikers in a drenching, rainbow-filled spray. (Beware of slippery stone steps.) The only downside: big crowds during peak season. On summer weekends, the hyper-popular Mist Trail can feel more like a trip to the mall than the Great Outdoors. But don't let that deter you. The Mist Trail remains one of Yosemite's all-time classic hikes. (Note: after reaching the top of Vernal Fall, strong hikers can continue to the top of 594-foot Nevada Fall, which adds 1.4 miles and 1,000 feet of elevation change to a round-trip hike from Happy Isles.)

TRAILHEAD The Mist Trail starts in Happy Isles (shuttle stop #16) at the eastern end of Yosemite Valley. From the shuttle stop, cross the stone bridge and follow the well-trodden path to your right.

◆ TRAIL INFO ◆

DIFFICULTY Strenuous	**HIKING TIME** 3–4 hours
DISTANCE 2.4 miles, round-trip	**ELEVATION CHANGE** 1,000 feet

Mist Trail

" How softly these rocks are adorned, and how fine and reassuring the company they keep, their feet among beautiful groves and meadows, their brows in the sky … bathed in floods of water, floods of light."

—John Muir

Nevada Fall

⊰ HALF DOME ⊱

SUMMARY   Half Dome is, without question, the most fabled hike in the park. This towering granite monolith beckons every adventurer who sets eyes on it. The challenging 8.5-mile trail to the summit starts in Yosemite Valley, passes Vernal Fall and Nevada Fall, then climbs to the base of Half Dome's steep backside. From there you'll haul yourself up a set of metal cables drilled into the rock—a vertigo-inducing experience sure to quicken your pulse. This is not a trail for the faint of heart. But if you've got the physical and mental stamina to conquer Half Dome, you'll be rewarded with jaw-dropping views of Yosemite Valley and the High Sierra. It's an experience you'll never forget. Strong hikers can make it round-trip in 12 hours. If you'd rather hike Half Dome in two days, you can camp at Little Yosemite Valley Campground, which is located about halfway to the top. See following pages for additional info.

TRAILHEAD   The most popular route to the top of Half Dome starts in Happy Isles (shuttle stop #16) and follows the Mist Trail (p.168) to the top of Nevada Fall. From there follow the signs to the top of Half Dome.

TRAIL INFO

DIFFICULTY Very strenuous   **HIKING TIME** 12–14 hours

DISTANCE 17 miles, round-trip   **ELEVATION CHANGE** 4,800 feet

HALF DOME INFO

Half Dome is one of America's most incredible hikes, but this 17-mile, 4,800-foot granite beast demands respect. Advance preparation is necessary.

CABLES

The final 700-foot ascent to the top of Half Dome is inclined between 45 and 60 degrees, which is far too steep to hike. Half Dome's unique cable system (photo p.178) puts the otherwise inaccessible peak within reach of strong hikers. Two sets of steel poles are placed in the rock at ten-foot intervals, and metal cables are strung between the poles. The cables are spaced 30 inches apart—small enough to grasp a cable with both hands, but large enough for two people to squeeze past one another. Smart hikers use rugged work gloves to protect their hands and enhance their grip. Wooden boards are laid flat between each set of poles, offering hikers a foothold to rest along the way. The cable system is installed in late May and removed in mid-October to protect it from winter damage. Exact dates vary based on seasonal weather conditions. Check the park's website for the most up-to-date info.

ONE DAY OR TWO?

It's possible to hike Half Dome in a single day, but only if you're an experienced hiker in great shape. I prefer splitting the long hike over two days, giving yourself plenty of time to enjoy the magnificent scenery. Overnight hikers can spend the night at Little Yosemite Valley Campground, which offers the closest backcountry camping to Half Dome. You'll need wilderness permits (p.18) to camp at Little Yosemite Valley, which is located one mile above Nevada Fall. There are food lockers, composting toilets, and a nearby stream for water. I like hiking to the campground on the first day, then heading up Half Dome early the next day.

CHOOSING THE BEST ROUTE

There are three popular routes to Half Dome, all of which converge at the top of Nevada Fall. The first route starts in Happy Isles and follows the Mist Trail to the top of Nevada Fall. The second route starts in Happy Isles and follows the John Muir Trail to the top of Nevada Fall. Although the Mist Trail is 1.5 miles shorter and more scenic than the John Muir Trail, the John Muir Trail has fewer crowds and a gentler uphill grade.

The third route starts at Glacier Point and follows the Panorama Trail to the top of Nevada Fall. This route is about two miles longer than Nevada Fall via the John Muir Trail, but because it starts at a higher elevation you'll save roughly 1,100 feet of climbing. Be aware that the Panorama Trail drops roughly 1,500 feet as it descends to Illilouette Falls—not bad on the way out, but a tough way to finish a long hike.

My favorite route starts at Glacier Point and finishes in Yosemite Valley. This requires catching the bus to Glacier Point (p.191) or shuttling two cars between Glacier Point and Yosemite Valley.

PERMITS

A maximum of 300 hikers (225 day hikers, 75 backpackers) are allowed on top of Half Dome each day. Permits for day hikers are distributed by lottery on recreation.gov. There is one pre-season permit lottery in March (weekend success rate: 2%, weekday success rate: 7%), plus daily lotteries for about 50 permits during hiking season (weekend success rate: 14%, weekday success rate: 32%). Backpackers should apply for Half Dome permits when they apply for Wilderness Permits (p.18). For comprehensive Half Dome permit info, visit the Yosemite National Park website.

WHAT'S ON TOP?

The top of Half Dome is a vast, mostly flat surface that's about the size of 17 football fields. Chipmunks and marmots are common, and the rare Mount Lyell salamander is sometimes spotted. Over half a dozen very small trees once grew on the summit, but most were chopped down and used for firewood when overnight camping was allowed on top of Half Dome. (Overnight camping was banned in 1993 due to the amount of human waste generated.)

DO NOT ASCEND THE CABLES IF DARK CLOUDS ARE VISIBLE!

Half Dome acts like a giant lightning rod during thunderstorms, and hikers on top have been killed by lightning strikes. A warning sign below the backside of Half Dome states: "DANGER. If a thunderstorm is anywhere on the horizon, do not pass beyond this sign. Lightning has struck Half Dome during every month of the year." A single bolt of lightning contains up to 100 million volts and reaches temperatures up to 55,000° F—five times hotter than the surface of the sun. Thunderstorms descend on Half Dome with remarkable speed, and you don't have to be on top to feel the effects. Rock climbers stranded on the sheer northwest face during thunderstorms have been shocked by lightning-induced electrical charges streaming across the wet granite, and hikers fleeing thunderstorms have been severely shocked while gripping Half Dome's metal cables.

DEATH ON HALF DOME

There have been over 20 recorded deaths on Half Dome. In 1972 a hiker on top of Half Dome took refuge from a lightning storm in a small cave. He was killed when lightning struck the cave. Thirteen years later, a group of young hikers ascended the cables during a lightning storm and sought refuge in the same cave. Lightning struck the cave again, killing one hiker and sending another into seizures that propelled him off the sheer northwest face.

Thousands of hikers use Half Dome's cables each year, but only five people have died while ascending or descending the cables. Many of these accidents occurred when the granite was slippery and wet. Other causes of death on Half Dome include suicides (6), falls while rock climbing (4), and unsuccessful BASE jumps (2).

Half Dome cables

View from Half Dome

⊰ FOUR MILE TRAIL ⊱

SUMMARY   Millions of tourists drive to Glacier Point to enjoy the stunning views 3,000 feet above Yosemite Valley, but those views are even more rewarding when you've earned them the hard way via the Four Mile Trail. This 4.8-mile trail (which originally measured four miles when the route was first constructed by James McCauley in the 1870s) is one of the best hikes in Yosemite Valley. It passes directly below Sentinel Rock and offers unrivaled views of Yosemite Falls. If hiking up 3,200 feet isn't your thing, consider riding the bus to Glacier Point (p.191) then hiking *down* 3,200 feet to Yosemite Valley. Conversely, if hiking just 9.2 miles isn't your thing, consider the following route: hike up the Four Mile Trail, hike down the Panorama Trail to the top of Nevada Fall, then hike down the Mist Trail (p.168) to Yosemite Valley. If you've got the time and the energy, the 14.5-mile Four Mile Trail/Panorama Trail/Mist Trail route is one of the finest hikes in the park.

TRAILHEAD   The Four Mile Trail starts between Sentinel Beach and Swinging Bridge on Southside Drive.

TRAIL INFO

DIFFICULTY Strenuous	**HIKING TIME** 6–8 hours
DISTANCE 9.6 miles, round-trip	**ELEVATION CHANGE** 3,200 feet

❧ YOSEMITE FALLS ᔆ

SUMMARY   If you love strenuous hikes and enormous waterfalls, it doesn't get better than hiking to the top of Yosemite Falls (p.132). Rising 2,600 feet in just 3.6 miles, the Yosemite Falls Trail features breathtaking views of Yosemite Valley, including Half Dome, Glacier Point, and up-close views of North America's tallest waterfall. From the trailhead it's roughly one mile and 80+ switchbacks to Columbia Point. Perched 1,000 feet above the floor of Yosemite Valley, Columbia Point offers panoramic views and makes a great destination for moderate hikers. A half-mile past Columbia Point you'll enjoy striking views of Upper Yosemite Fall. The rest of the trail is steep, rocky, and strenuous, but you'll revel in fabulous scenery as you huff and puff to the top. The trail ends at a fenced-in ledge along the lip of Upper Yosemite Fall. The Yosemite Falls Trail is most spectacular in May and June, when Yosemite Falls is flowing at its peak.

TRAILHEAD   The trail to the top of Yosemite Falls starts at Camp 4. Take the shuttle to Yosemite Lodge (stop #7), and cross the street to Camp 4. The hike starts between the parking area and the campground.

TRAIL INFO	
DIFFICULTY Strenuous	**HIKING TIME** 6–8 hours
DISTANCE 7.2 miles, round-trip	**ELEVATION CHANGE** 2,700 feet

"It is in no scene or scenes the chasm consists, but in the miles of scenery where cliffs of awful height and rocks of vast magnitude and of varied and exquisite coloring, are banked and fringed and draped and shadowed by the tender foliage of noble and lovely trees ... associated with the most tranquil meadows, the most playful streams, and every variety of soft and peaceful pastoral beauty."

—Frederick Law Olmstead

GLACIER POINT ROAD

★ ★ ★ ★ ★

Half Dome at Sunset

GLACIER POINT ROAD

THIS 16-MILE ROAD wraps around Yosemite Valley's south rim on its way to Glacier Point, one of the most stunning and accessible viewpoints in the park. Perched 3,200 feet above the floor of Yosemite Valley, Glacier Point offers jaw-dropping views of Half Dome and a panorama of Sierra spectacles: Yosemite Falls, North Dome, Clouds Rest, Tenaya Canyon, the Royal Arches. Thanks to its high elevation and dark night skies, Glacier Point is also one of California's top stargazing destinations. Even if you're only in Yosemite for a single day, no first-time visitor should leave without enjoying the views from Glacier Point.

Most people drive to Glacier Point, revel in the scenery, then turn around and drive back. There's nothing wrong with that, but if you've got the time Glacier Point Road has plenty more to offer. A handful of trails venture along Yosemite Valley's south rim, showcasing fabulous viewpoints that are far less crowded than Glacier Point. Free ranger programs include natural history walks, sunset talks, and astronomy programs (check the *Yosemite Guide* for dates and times). Want to spend more than an afternoon exploring the area? Consider spending the night at Bridalveil Creek Campground (p.38), located just off Glacier Point Road.

Glacier Point is roughly 30 road miles from Yosemite Valley (about an hour drive one-way). Don't feel like driving? A four-hour Glacier Point Bus Tour departs Yosemite Valley at 8:30am and 1:30pm daily from late May through October ($57 adult, $37 child, travelyosemite.com). You can also ride the bus one-way to Glacier Point ($29 adult, $18 child), then hike down to Yosemite Valley via the Four Mile Trail (p.182) or the Panorama Trail, which heads to Nevada Fall and the Mist Trail (p.168).

In winter and early spring, the last ten miles of Glacier Point Road are closed due to heavy snow. The first six miles are plowed as far as Badger Pass Ski Area, California's oldest downhill ski resort. Free winter shuttles run between Yosemite Valley hotels and Badger Pass, where you can also enjoy cross-country skiing and snowshoeing. Cross-country skiers can explore dozens of miles of nearby trails or plan an overnight trip to Glacier Point or Ostrander Lake, both of which offer overnight accommodations (p.28). Note: four-wheel drive or tire chains are required for all vehicles driving to Badger Pass in winter.

Badger Pass Ski Area

Open since 1933, Badger Pass is the oldest ski resort in California. It's also the birthplace of snowboarding, which was first attempted here in 1938 when Honolulu reporter Robert Trumbull visited with a customized board and went "snurfing" (snow surfing). Today there are five lifts and ten runs for skiers and snowboarders. Easy terrain, short lift lines, and relatively cheap tickets make Badger Pass great for families and beginners. Cross-country skiers enjoy 90 miles of marked trails and 25 miles of machine-groomed track. Ski season generally runs mid-December to late March, depending on seasonal weather conditions. A small base lodge offers food, drinks, equipment rentals, and ski instruction. Lift tickets: $62 adults, $35 kids (209-372-1000, travelyosemite.com).

Clark Range View

This small roadside pullout offers great views of the Clark Range, one of Yosemite's most rugged and remote mountain ranges. In the foreground is Mt. Starr King, a conical granite dome that rises to a maximum elevation of 9,092 feet. The dome is named for Thomas Starr King, a famous Unitarian minister who visited Yosemite Valley in the 1860s and preached about its beauty. Beyond Mt. Starr King is 11,522-foot Mt. Clark, the highest peak in the Clark Range. Both the peak and the range are named after Galen Clark, the first Guardian of Yosemite (p.98). Exploring the Clark Range requires several days of intense backpacking, but it contains some of the most beautiful scenery in the park (p.210).

Washburn Point

This large turnout features a stunning view framed by Half Dome on the left and Mt. Starr King on the right. In the center is Merced Canyon, home to two of the park's most impressive waterfalls: Nevada Fall (594 feet) and Vernal Fall (317 feet). In spring, when the Merced River is swollen with snowmelt, the roar of these two waterfalls reaches all the way to Washburn Point.

Moments before the Merced River tumbles down Nevada Fall, the water is churned and frothed by a series of violent rapids, giving the waterfall a brilliant white color that inspired early explorers to name it Nevada (Spanish for "snowfall"). Vernal Fall, below, was named for its "cool, vernal spray." You can view both waterfalls up close along the popular Mist Trail (p.168).

The view from Washburn Point reveals that Half Dome isn't actually half of a dome. In fact, more than 70% of the dome remains intact. Half Dome's unique shape formed over millions of years due to the exfoliation of overlying rock layers. Later, during the Ice Age, glaciers chipped away its steep northwest face, giving it the impression of "half of a dome" from the floor of Yosemite Valley.

"[Half Dome] strikes even the most casual observer as a new revelation in mountain forms; its existence would be considered an impossibility if it were not there before us in all its reality; it is a unique thing in mountain scenery, and nothing even approaching it can be found except in the Sierra Nevada."

—Josiah Whitney

Washburn Point

Glacier Point

The sweeping views from 7,214-foot Glacier Point are arguably the best in Yosemite. Nearly all of Yosemite Valley's famous landmarks can be seen in a single panorama, including three glorious waterfalls (Yosemite Falls, Nevada Fall, and Vernal Fall). Towering above them all is Half Dome, which rises 1,628 feet above Glacier Point.

To get to Glacier Point, follow the short, paved path from the large parking area. Along the way you'll pass an outdoor amphitheater, the Glacier Point Snack Shop (which doubles as a winter lodge for cross-country skiers), and a small Geology Hut that explains the story behind the scenery. Just below the Geology Hut is a pair of giant binoculars—great for spotting ant-like hikers on top of Half Dome—and a metal plaque pointing out famous landmarks and distant peaks. Glacier Point itself is a small platform, surrounded by a protective railing, perched 3,214 feet above Curry Village on the floor of Yosemite Valley.

At night, Glacier Point's high elevation, clean air, and lack of light pollution make it one of the best stargazing destinations in California. Rangers offer free

Stars Over Yosemite astronomy programs on summer weekends, and on summer Saturdays amateur astronomy clubs set up telescopes for public viewing. If you visit Sunday through Thursday, you can sign up for a paid Starry Night Skies Over Yosemite program that includes transportation from Yosemite Valley ($67 adults/$47 kids, $10 without transportation, travelyosemite.com).

No matter when you visit, you'll enjoy incredible views of Half Dome, which dominates the northeast skyline. Behind Half Dome is a striking granite mountain called Clouds Rest. Although Half Dome appears higher from Glacier Point, Clouds Rest is actually over 1,000 feet higher than Half Dome. The western side of Clouds Rest, which is almost entirely bare granite, tumbles down into Tenaya Canyon, which has been called the "Bermuda Triangle of Yosemite" because so many hikers get lost there.

Until 1882 Glacier Point was only accessible via the Four Mile Trail from Yosemite Valley. The trail was built in 1871 by James McCauley, and for years he charged a toll of $1 per hiker. In 1878 McCauley opened the Mountain House Hotel at Glacier Point, which was joined by the Glacier Point Hotel in 1917. Sadly, both structures burned down in 1969, and neither was rebuilt.

~ SENTINEL DOME ~

SUMMARY This short, rewarding hike offers plenty of bang for your buck. At 8,122 feet, Sentinel Dome is the second-highest point above the rim of Yosemite Valley (after Half Dome). Perched 1,000 feet higher than Glacier Point, Sentinel Dome has panoramic views that include Half Dome, Yosemite Valley, and over a dozen High Sierra peaks, which can be identified using a metal plaque embedded in a boulder at the summit. Not far from the plaque is the fallen skeleton of a gnarled Jeffrey pine. This wind-contorted tree, made famous by Ansel Adams, was over 400 years old when it died during a drought in the mid-1970s. Remarkably, the skeleton remained standing until 2003. Sentinel Dome makes a fantastic sunset destination for anyone looking to escape the crowds at Glacier Point. As Dr. Joseph LeConte put it after witnessing a sunset from Sentinel Dome in 1870: "Such a sunset, combined with such a view, I never imagined."

TRAILHEAD The Sentinel Dome Trail starts from Taft Point/Sentinel Dome parking area (14 miles east of Chinquapin; 7 miles west of Glacier Point). The parking area is easily identified by its open setting and small restroom.

◀ TRAIL INFO ▶

RATING Moderate

HIKING TIME 1 hour

DISTANCE 2.2 miles, round-trip

ELEVATION CHANGE 380 feet

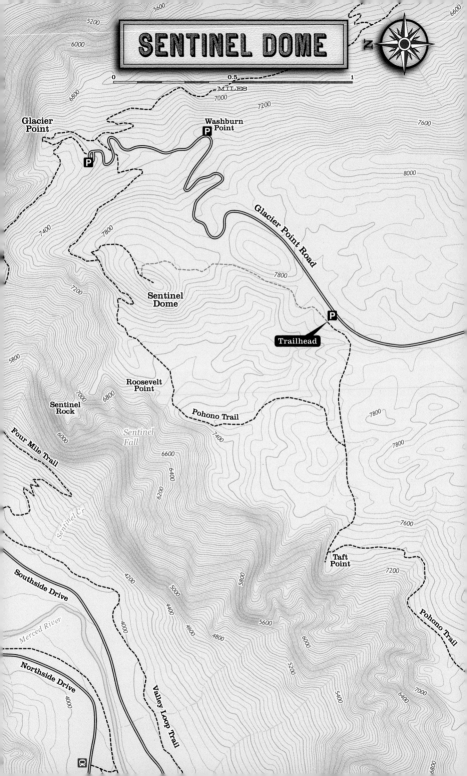

~∂ TAFT POINT ⌐~

SUMMARY This easy hike drops down from Glacier Point Road, twists through a beautiful pine forest, and ends at a dramatic granite ledge. A high point on the ledge marks Taft Point, a vertigo-inducing precipice 3,400 feet above the floor of Yosemite Valley. A small metal railing is all that protects you from free fall. Taft Point (7,503 feet) offers great views of Yosemite Falls, but sensational views of El Capitan are what really sets the viewpoint apart. A short distance from the viewpoint are The Fissures, natural cracks in the granite that plummet hundreds of feet straight down. Watch your step! And note how some of the fissures have large rocks lodged in their narrow openings. Taft Point is named for President William Taft, who hiked along Yosemite Valley's south rim with John Muir in 1909. The 340-pound Taft later remarked of the experience: "While I am tired from the open air exercise, I feel greatly the better for it."

TRAILHEAD The Taft Point Trail starts from Taft Point/Sentinel Dome parking area (14 miles east of Chinquapin; 2 miles west of Glacier Point). The parking area is easily noticed by its open setting and small restroom.

TRAIL INFO

RATING Easy

DISTANCE 2.2 miles, round-trip

HIKING TIME 1–2 hours

ELEVATION CHANGE 250 feet

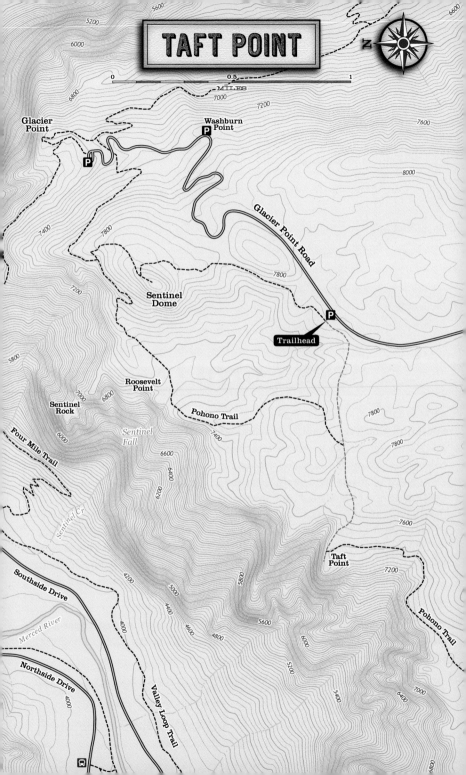

✌ OSTRANDER LAKE ᔬ

SUMMARY   Most hikers who visit Glacier Point Road gravitate to trails along the rim that offer spectacular views of Yosemite Valley. But this beautiful lake, nestled among sparkling granite slopes, is a terrific destination if you're afraid of heights or looking to escape the crowds. From the trailhead you'll pass through 2.5 miles of relatively flat terrain. Bear left at the first trail junction (1.4 miles), then left again at the second trail junction (2.7 miles). Next, prepare yourself for the trail's most difficult stretch: a 1,500-foot vertical ascent. Towards the top of the climb you'll skirt Horizon Ridge, which offers great views of Mount Starr King, the Illilouette Creek Basin, and the Clark Range beyond. After peaking at 8,720 feet, the trails drops down 200 feet to Ostrander Lake. On the lake's northern shore lies Ostrander Ski Hut, a rustic stone building where cross-country skiers can spend the night in winter (p.28).

TRAILHEAD   The Ostrander Lake trailhead starts from the Ostrander Lake parking area (9 miles east of Chinquapin; 7 miles south of Glacier Point). Restrooms are available at the parking area.

◆ TRAIL INFO ◆

RATING Moderate	**HIKING TIME** 6–8 hours
DISTANCE 11.4 miles, round-trip	**ELEVATION CHANGE** 1,720 feet

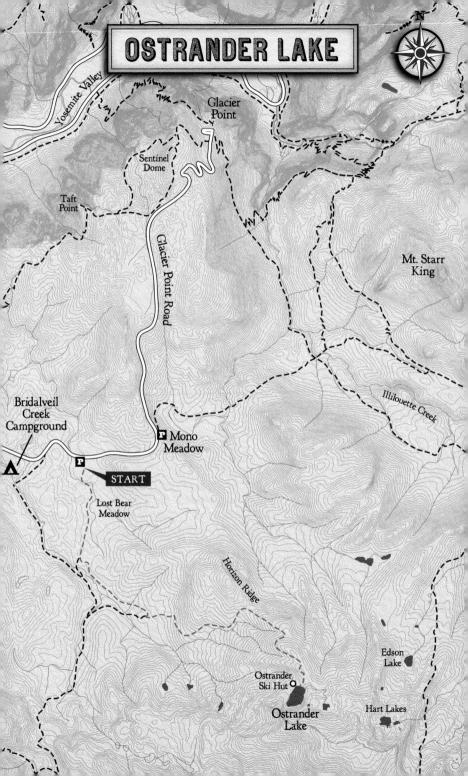

OSTRANDER LAKE

N

Yosemite Valley

Glacier Point

Sentinel Dome

Taft Point

Glacier Point Road

Mt. Starr King

Illilouette Creek

Bridalveil Creek Campground

P Mono Meadow

P
START

Lost Bear Meadow

Horizon Ridge

Edson Lake

Ostrander Ski Hut ○

Ostrander Lake

Hart Lakes

~☙ POHONO TRAIL ❧~

SUMMARY On busy weekends, when Yosemite is teeming with visitors, the Pohono Trail offers hikers a well-earned sense of solitude. Despite its breathtaking views of Bridalveil Fall, Ribbon Fall, and El Capitan, the Pohono Trail remains relatively uncrowded. While other tourists are circling parking lots in Yosemite Valley, you can enjoy the Pohono Trail's unspoiled grandeur on a day hike or overnight backpack. Although the complete 13.8-mile Pohono Trail stretches from Tunnel View (p.144) to Taft Point (p.202), you can reach the most spectacular viewpoints—Dewey Point (above), Crocker Point, Stanford Point—via a 1.8-mile hike from Glacier Point Road. The hiking distance listed below is for a round-trip hike from the McGurk Meadow trailhead to Stanford Point. A round-trip hike to Dewey Point is 8.2 miles.

TRAILHEAD The McGurk Meadow trailhead is located 7.5 miles from the start of Glacier Point Road on the left. (Park in the pullout 100 yards up the road.) Follow the trail 1.9 miles to the junction of the Pohono Trail and turn left towards Dewey Point. Note: overnight camping is not allowed to the right of the junction.

◄ TRAIL INFO ►

RATING Moderate

DISTANCE 10.5 miles, round-trip

HIKING TIME 4 hours

ELEVATION CHANGE 540 feet

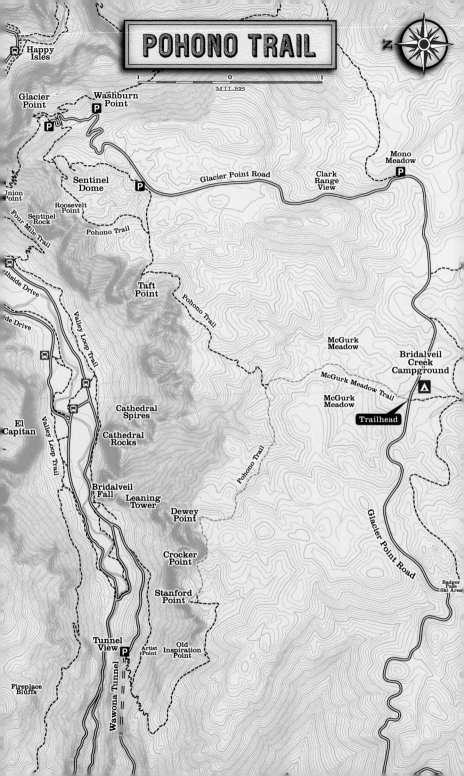

Dewey Point

⊰ THE CLARK RANGE ⊱

SUMMARY For serious backpackers who aren't afraid of multiple days in the wilderness—and several thousand feet of elevation change—few hikes in the park are as rewarding as the Clark Range. Seldom visited due to its remote, rugged terrain, the Clark Range features pristine alpine lakes, dramatic landscapes above treeline, and the highest pass in the park: Red Peak Pass (11,200 feet). Highlights along the trail include Ottoway Lakes, Red Peak Pass, and gorgeous Red Devil Lake, where enchanting granite shores offer stunning views of the Clark Range during the day and fabulous stargazing at night. To finish off the trip in style, reserve a tent cabin at Merced High Sierra Camp and treat yourself to a bed, a hot shower, and a home-cooked meal on your last night. Finish the hike by heading down the Mist Trail to Happy Isles in Yosemite Valley.

TRAILHEAD The Clark Range hike starts at the Mono Meadows trailhead off Glacier Point Road. Unless you have two cars to shuttle between the start and the finish, leave your car in Yosemite Valley and ride the Glacier Point bus (p.125) to the Mono Meadows trailhead.

TRAIL INFO

RATING Very strenuous	**HIKING TIME** 6–7 days
DISTANCE 46.5 miles	**ELEVATION CHANGE** 7,000 feet

Hiking below Red Peak Pass

Red Devil Lake

Merced Grove

BIG OAK FLAT ROAD

THIS 17-MILE ROAD, which stretches between the park's Big Oak Flat Entrance and Yosemite Valley, offers the most direct route to Yosemite Valley if you're traveling from San Francisco. There's little dramatic scenery past the entrance station, but the Merced Grove of giant sequoias (below) is certainly worth a visit. Two campgrounds are located along Big Oak Flat Road: Crane Flat and Hodgdon Meadow. Both are located far from Yosemite's popular sights, but they might be your best bet for an open campsite during peak season.

Eight miles past Big Oak Flat Entrance is Crane Flat. Named for the sandhill cranes that early explorers found here, Crane Flat was the site of a rowdy saloon in the late 1800s. Back then visiting sheepherders drowned their loneliness in whiskey. Today Crane Flat sells an even more addictive liquid: gasoline. As the only "reasonably" priced gas station anywhere near Yosemite Valley, Crane Flat is one of the most logistically important points in the park—particularly if you're about to embark on the long drive up 46-mile Tioga Road (p.221). Adjacent to the gas station is a convenience store with cold drinks and snacks.

Southeast of Crane Flat the road descends roughly 12 miles towards Yosemite Valley—and the views grow more and more dramatic with each passing mile. The final descent into the Merced River Canyon offers fabulous glimpses of Half Dome, El Capitan, and Bridalveil Fall. Scenic pullouts on the side of the road offer great opportunities to stop and enjoy the views. At the end of the descent, Big Oak Flat Road intersects with Highway 140, which heads into Yosemite Valley.

Merced Grove

Home to about two dozen giant sequoias (p.72), Merced Grove is the smallest and least crowded of Yosemite's three sequoia groves. The big trees are reached via a 1.5-mile trail, which descends nearly 600 feet from the parking area. The steep hike can be strenuous. Plan on at least two to three hours for a visit, and bring plenty of water (there's no water at the grove). The Merced Grove parking area is located about 14 miles from Yosemite Valley (30-minute drive) and 5.5 miles from Big Oak Flat Entrance (ten-minute drive).

TIOGA ROAD

★ ★ ★ ★ ★

Clouds Rest from Olmstead Point

TIOGA ROAD

THIS 46-MILE ROAD rises high into the heart of Yosemite's High Sierra, climbing 3,750 feet and revealing some of the finest alpine scenery in the park. After visiting Yosemite Valley and Glacier Point, Tioga Road should be next on your list. Highlights include Olmstead Point, a dramatic viewpoint with bold perspectives of Clouds Rest and Half Dome, and Tenaya Lake, whose icy waters reflect fabulous granite domes. Past Tenaya Lake, Tioga Road skirts Tuolumne Meadows (p.247), then climbs to Tioga Pass—at 9,941 feet, the highest paved road in California. The road then exits the park and plunges more than 3,000 feet to the eastern base of the Sierra Nevada Mountains.

In winter Tioga Road closes due to heavy snow. When the first significant snow falls (generally around mid-November) Tioga Road shuts down. Its reopening date depends on winter snowfall. Tioga Road often opens around mid-May, but following extremely snowy winters it can stay closed until early July.

Tioga Road begins its ascent at Crane Flat, 16 miles northwest of Yosemite Valley along Big Oak Flat Road (Highway 120). Crane Flat's gas station is a good place to fill up if your tank is running low. There's also a small convenience store.

Just beyond Crane Flat is the Tuolumne Grove of giant sequoias, Yosemite's second-largest sequoia grove. Past Tuolumne Grove, Tioga Road rises through an impressive forest, passing turnoffs for multiple campgrounds and White Wolf Lodge, which offers the only overnight lodging between Yosemite Valley and Tuolumne Meadows. Eventually the forest gives way to dramatic mountain views, which become increasingly dramatic as you climb higher and higher.

Tioga Road offers access to some of the finest hikes and backpacks in Yosemite, including Clouds Rest, 10 Lakes, and two popular High Sierra Camps: May Lake and Sunrise. Another great option is hiking down to North Dome, which is perched on the north rim of Yosemite Valley.

Throughout summer a shuttle runs between Olmstead Point and Tioga Pass (check the *Yosemite Guide* for current schedules). There's also the seasonal Yosemite Valley to Tuolumne Meadows Hikers Bus, which makes daily trips along Tioga Road and stops at popular trailheads along the way ($23 round-trip, $14.50 one-way, 888-413-8869, travelyosemite.com).

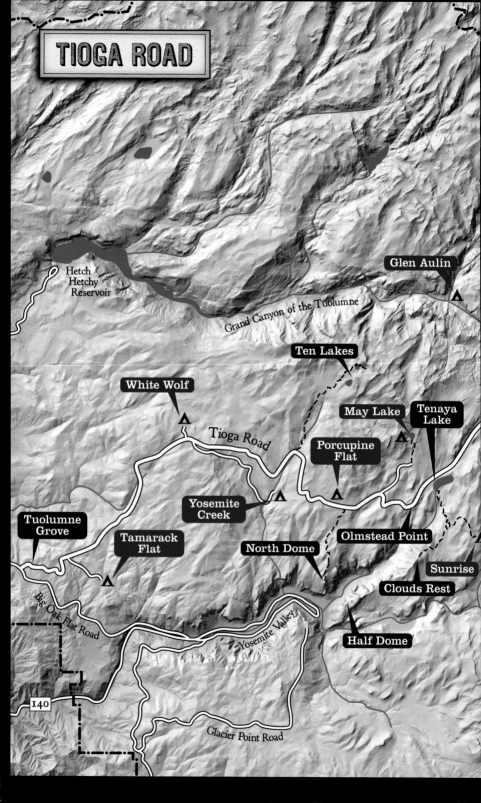

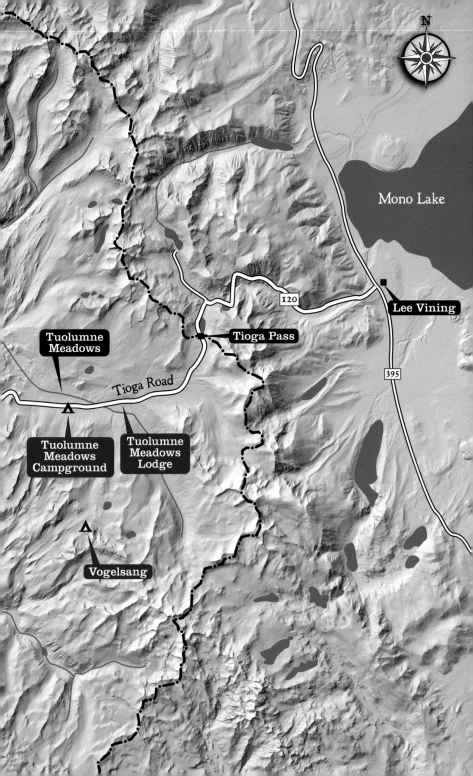

Tuolumne Grove

Home to roughly 45 giant sequoias (p.72), the Tuolumne Grove is the second-largest sequoia grove in Yosemite. Although overshadowed by the larger and more famous Mariposa Grove, the Tuolumne Grove is worth a visit if you're enchanted by big trees. The grove is located roughly half a mile past Crane Flat junction. A two-mile round-trip path starts from the parking area and drops about 500 feet. Among the notable specimens: a sequoia with a walking tunnel cut through the trunk (the tunnel was cut in 1878), and a sequoia that rises nearly 300 feet—one of the tallest giant sequoias in the world.

Olmstead Point

Olmstead Point is the most dramatic viewpoint on Tioga Road. Dominating the southern horizon is Clouds Rest, a 9,926-foot mountain with billowing granite slopes. Just west of Clouds Rest is an unusual look at Half Dome's backside. East of Clouds Rest lies Tenaya Lake. During the Ice Age, a massive glacier flowed from Tenaya Lake into Yosemite Valley, passing Clouds Rest and Half Dome along the way. Olmstead Point was also buried under the glacier, which smoothed and polished the bedrock. When the glacier melted, boulders embedded in the ice settled on the bedrock, and these boulders, called glacial erratics, are still visible today. The quarter-mile geology trail that starts at Olmstead Point passes some fine examples of glacial erratics.

Half Dome from Olmstead Point

Clouds Rest & Half Dome

"Clouds Rest was fairly enveloped in drifting gossamer films, and the Half Dome loomed up in the garish light like a majestic, living creature clad in the same gauzy, wind-woven drapery."

—John Muir

Tenaya Lake

Lying at an elevation of 8,149 feet, this stunning alpine lake is a great place to take a break and bask in the glorious scenery. Several picnic areas are located alongside the road, and an easy two-mile trail skirts the lake's southern shore. You can pick up the trail from the sandy beach at the eastern end of the lake. This natural beach, a popular destination on hot summer days, is the result of winter freeze-thaw cycles. When the lake freezes, cracks form in the ice that fill with water on warm days. When temperatures drop below freezing, the water in the cracks freezes and expands, pushing the previously formed ice towards the shore. As the ice pushes outward it picks up sediment on the bottom of the lake and pushes it towards the shore, forming the sandy beach.

Like many lakes in the Sierra Nevada, Tenaya Lake formed when a massive glacier scooped out a basin in the bedrock. In the depths of the Ice Age, the ice here was over 2,000 feet deep. When the glacier melted, the basin filled with water to form Tenaya Lake, which has a maximum depth of 180 feet today. The southwest end of the lake still remains partially dammed by debris left in the glacier's wake.

The Ahwahneechee call this lake *Pywiack*, "Lake of Shining Rocks." The name Tenaya was given by the Mariposa Battalion, a local militia organized by white settlers to remove the Ahwahneechee from the mountains. On May 22, 1851, the Battalion captured several dozen Ahwahneechee hiding near the shores of Pywiack. After marching the Ahwahneechee out of the mountains, Battalion members named the lake "Tenaya" after the chief of the tribe.

Our camp at Lake Tenaya was especially memorable. After supper and some talk by the fire, LeConte and I sauntered through the pine groves to the shore and sat down on a big rock that stands out a little way in the water. The full moon and the stars filled the lake with light ... Subsiding waves made gentle heaving swells, and a slight breeze ruffled the surface, giving rise to ever-changing pictures of wondrous brightness. At first we talked freely, admiring the silvery masses and ripples of light, and the mystic, wavering dance of the stars and rocks and shadows reflected in the unstable mirror. But soon came perfect stillness, earth and sky were inseparably blended and spiritualized, and we could only gaze on the celestial vision in devout, silent, wondering admiration.

—John Muir

⊰ NORTH DOME ⊱

SUMMARY   Most hikes to the rim of Yosemite Valley start on the floor of Yosemite Valley and require hiking *up* several thousand feet. But North Dome is reached via a one-way, 5.2-mile trail that drops *down* 600 feet from Tioga Road. You'll still have to hike 600 feet up on the return (with a few extra ups and downs thrown in for good measure), but the effort is more than worth it. From the top of 7,542-foot North Dome you'll be treated to sweeping views of Yosemite Valley. Most impressive are the striking views of Half Dome's sheer 2,000-foot northwest face, which dominates the eastern horizon. Although normally done as a day hike, North Dome also makes a great overnight backpack. The forested recess behind North Dome has several great campsites, and sunsets here are among the most spectacular in the park. Backpacking note: there is no water near North Dome. Plan on filling up your water bottles at one of the several streams you'll pass early in the hike.

TRAILHEAD   North Dome's trailhead is located at Porcupine Creek (25 miles east of Crane Flat; 15 miles west of Tuolumne Meadows).

◢ TRAIL INFO ◣

RATING Moderate	**HIKING TIME** 4–5 hours
DISTANCE 10.4 miles, round-trip	**ELEVATION CHANGE** 600 feet

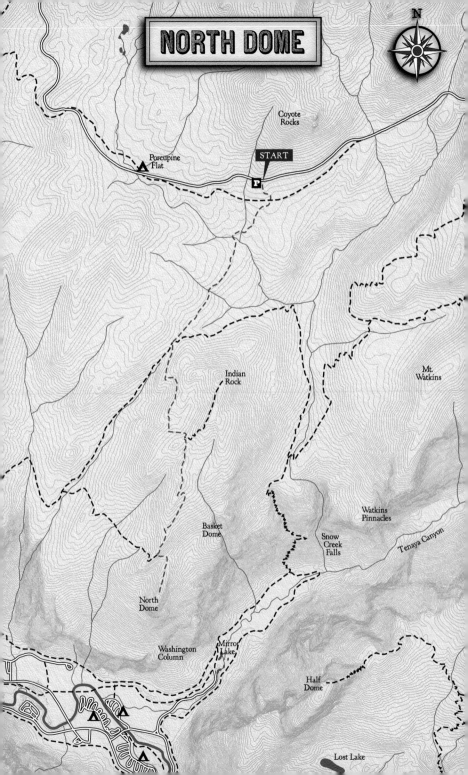

Half Dome

Granite Domes

North Dome (right) and Half Dome (left) are classic examples of Yosemite's famous granite domes. The domes formed when previously overlying rocks eroded along concentric cracks, flaking off like layers of an onion. But why are the domes bare when the surrounding landscape is covered with trees? A phenomenon called "ice creep" is partly responsible for the absence of vegetation. When winter snow accumulates, the bottom-most layers compress into ice. As sunlight warms the snow, water seeps under the ice and lubricates the rock. The snowpack then slides down the granite and scrapes away accumulated soil and vegetation. Although a few cracks in the granite retain enough soil for some plants to grow, most of the dome remains bare.

North Dome

⊰ MAY LAKE ⊱

SUMMARY   May Lake is Yosemite's most accessible High Sierra Camp. The trail to the lake is just one mile long with only 400 feet of elevation change. Even if you haven't booked a night at one of the cozy High Sierra tent cabins, this gorgeous alpine lake (elevation: 9,350 feet) still makes a great day hike or overnight backpack. Looming 1,500 feet above the lake is 10,850-foot Mount Hoffman, the geographic center of Yosemite National Park. Although there's no official trail to the top, Mt. Hoffman's summit is a popular destination reached by an unofficial two-mile trail. If you're comfortable hiking off trail and feel like you can handle the strenuous ascent, Mount Hoffman is a classic destination with fabulous 360-degree views. As John Muir put it when describing how best to spend one's time in Yosemite: "Go straight to Mt. Hoffman ... From the summit nearly all the Yosemite park is displayed like a map."

TRAILHEAD   Turn onto May Lake Road (27 miles east of Crane Flat; 20 miles west of Tuolumne Meadows) and follow the road two miles to the trailhead.

TRAIL INFO

RATING Easy	**HIKING TIME** 2 hours
DISTANCE 2 miles, round-trip	**ELEVATION CHANGE** 400 feet

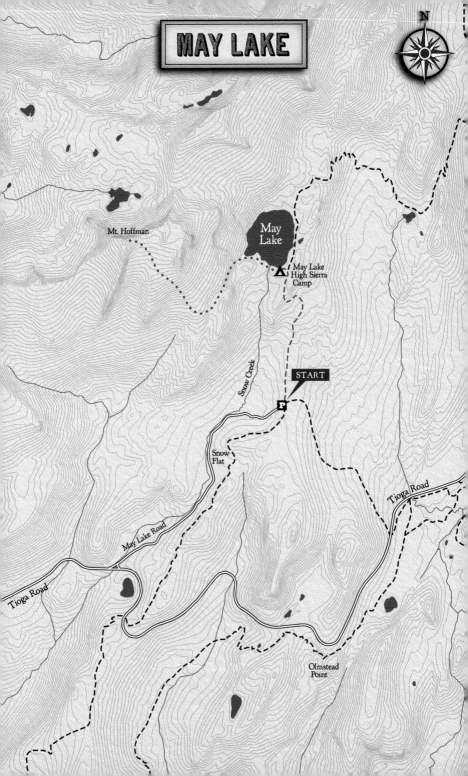

~ CLOUDS REST ~

SUMMARY   Thousands of ambitious hikers set their sights on Half Dome, but savvy Yosemite connoisseurs know that 9,926-foot Clouds Rest offers better views in a shorter distance with fewer crowds. Nothing against Half Dome—it still offers fantastic views of Yosemite Valley—but Clouds Rest offers great views of Yosemite Valley, plus amazing views of the High Sierra, *plus* incredible views 1,000 feet above Half Dome! Simply put: Clouds Rest is one of the best hikes in Yosemite. The trail starts near the southwest shore of Tenaya Lake. After roughly 1.5 miles the trail rises up a steep, 1,000-foot slope filled with switchbacks. This is the hardest part of the hike. From there it's a nice stroll through the forest before the final, dramatic push to Clouds Rest, which follows a narrow ridge with steep dropoffs. Although Clouds Rest is easily done in a day, there are several good campsites for backpackers along the trail.

TRAILHEAD   The trail to Clouds Rest starts at the Sunrise Lakes Trailhead at the southwest end of Tenaya Lake. After reaching the top of the steep ascent, the trail splits. Follow the signs to Clouds Rest.

TRAIL INFO

RATING Strenuous   **HIKING TIME** 7–8 hours

DISTANCE 14 miles, round-trip   **ELEVATION CHANGE** 1,780 feet

View from Clouds Rest

⁓ SUNRISE ⁓

SUMMARY The lush meadow at Sunrise High Sierra Camp offers weary hikers the ultimate in alpine relaxation. Although often waterlogged and spongy in early summer, by mid-summer it's a wildflower-strewn paradise with a serpentine creek flowing through the center. Lovely views of the surrounding granite peaks leave no doubt as to why Sunrise Meadow was included on the John Muir Trail. Even without the lure of Sunrise High Sierra Camp, Sunrise Meadow would still be a popular backpacking destination. Several exceptional campsites are perched on a rise overlooking the meadow, and campers are treated to (drum roll, please!) composting toilets.

TRAILHEAD The most direct route to Sunrise High Sierra Camp (info listed below) starts at the Sunrise Lakes Trailhead at the southwest end of Tenaya Lake. An alternate route starts in Tuolumne Meadows at the Cathedral Lakes Trailhead (p.258) and follows the John Muir Trail down to Sunrise Meadow. Although easier, the Cathedral Lake route is slightly longer (13.2 miles round-trip, 1,300 feet elevation change).

TRAIL INFO

RATING Strenuous

DISTANCE 10.4 miles, round-trip

HIKING TIME 6–7 hours

ELEVATION CHANGE 1,600 feet

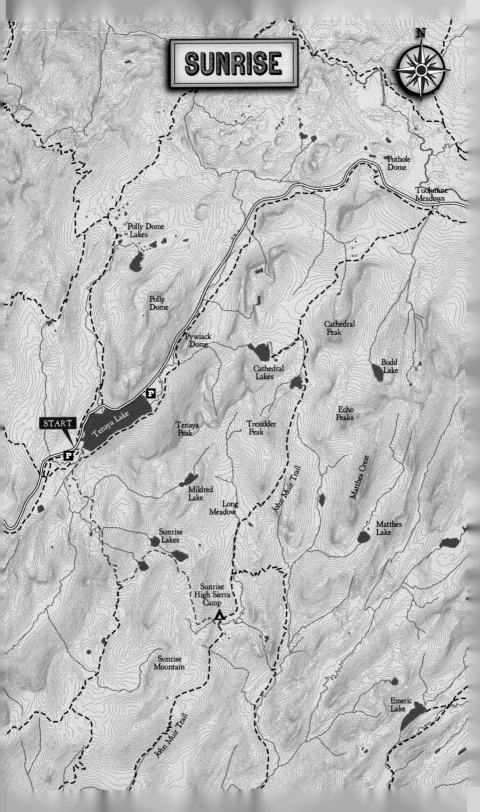

❧ TEN LAKES ❧

SUMMARY This secluded cluster of lakes is nestled in a granite basin at about 9,000 feet. Despite the name, there are only seven lakes at Ten Lakes (three previously counted bodies of water are now considered ponds). Numerical shortfall aside, Ten Lakes makes a good, long day hike and a superb overnight backpack. There's great fishing, and because the lakes lie below 9,600, feet campfires are allowed at night. The trail to Ten Lakes climbs gradually to Half Moon Meadow, then makes a steep ascent to 9,500-foot Ten Lakes Pass. At the top of the pass you'll be treated to terrific views of the High Sierra, including Mt. Conness and the Sawtooth Ridge. From Ten Lakes Pass descend 500 feet into Ten Lakes Basin. A few hundred yards north of the lakes, the outer rim of Ten Lakes Basin drops thousands of feet into the Grand Canyon of the Tuolumne River (p.284).

TRAILHEAD The hike starts at the Ten Lakes trailhead (20 miles east of Crane Flat; 26 miles west of Tuolumne Meadows). A good-sized parking area is located across the road from the trailhead.

◣ TRAIL INFO ◢

RATING Strenuous

DISTANCE 11.8 miles, round-trip

HIKING TIME 6–7 hours

ELEVATION CHANGE 2,000 feet

TUOLUMNE
MEADOWS

★ ★ ★ ★ ★

Tuolumne Meadows & Mount Conness

TUOLUMNE MEADOWS

LYING AT AN elevation of 8,600 feet, Tuolumne Meadows is the gateway to Yosemite's High Sierra—a stunning alpine wilderness of snow-capped peaks, wildflower-strewn meadows, and miles of sparkling granite. Hiking trails radiate out from Tuolumne (pronounced *too-ALL-uh-me*), offering hikers and rock climbers access to Yosemite's outdoor wonderland. Whether you're looking for an easy stroll, a moderate day hike, or a strenuous week-long backpack, Tuolumne Meadows has it all. It's also the Sierra Nevada's largest subalpine meadow, making it a great place to just kick back and relax.

For thousands of years, the Ahwahneechee journeyed from Yosemite Valley to Tuolumne Meadows to trade with the Mono tribe, who lived in the deserts east of Yosemite. Tuolumne's high elevation offered both the Ahwahneechee and the Mono relief from the summer heat.

Fast forward to the present ... and not much has changed. In July and August, when Yosemite Valley is hot and crowded, savvy visitors head to Tuolumne Meadows to cool off and relax. Temperatures in Tuolumne Meadows are generally 15 to 20 degrees cooler than in Yosemite Valley. And while not entirely uncrowded, Tuolumne Meadows never feels like a carnival. Regardless, true Sierra solitude is never more than a hike away. (Sweaty hiker note: hot showers are available at Tuolumne Meadows Lodge for a small fee.)

When it comes to Tuolumne hiking, timing is key. In winter Tuolumne Meadows is often buried under 10–12 feet of snow. Visit in early spring and many trails might still be covered in snow. Visit just after the snow melts and you'll be fighting off swarms of mosquitoes. Visit after the mosquitoes die down, however, and you'll be treated to High Sierra splendor. Check Yosemite's official website (nps.gov/yose) for current trail conditions, and ask rangers about mosquitoes before hitting the trail. August and September are consistently good months for Tuolumne hiking, but September usually brings the first frost. By late September, nights in Tuolumne often dip below freezing.

No matter when you visit Tuolumne, plan on bringing warm clothes. Summer days are famously sunny and warm, but nights can get chilly. There have even been snow flurries in July! Also be aware that afternoon thundershowers, though infrequent, are always possible.

Tuolumne Meadows
BASICS

Getting to Tuolumne Meadows

Located along Tioga Road, Tuolumne Meadows is 55 miles (90-minute drive) from Yosemite Valley and 13 miles (30-minute drive) from the town of Lee Vining at the eastern base of the Sierra Nevada. The Yosemite Valley to Tuolumne Meadows Hikers Bus makes daily trips during peak season ($23 round-trip, $14.50 one-way, 888-413-8869, travelyosemite.com). YARTS (Yosemite Area Regional Transportation System, 877-989-2787, yarts.com) offers a seasonal shuttle between Mammoth Mountain and Yosemite Valley that stops in Tuolumne Meadows.

Getting Around Tuolumne Meadows

During peak season a paid shuttle runs between Olmstead Point and Tioga Pass (check the *Yosemite Guide* for seasonal schedules).

Services

TUOLUMNE MEADOWS VISITOR CENTER

This small visitor center is a great place for up-to-date Tuolumne info: trail conditions, shuttle schedules, weather reports, etc. There are also natural history exhibits and a small bookstore. Open through late September (209-372-0263).

WILDERNESS CENTER

Pick up wilderness permits at this small building, located half a mile east of Tuolumne Campground, just off Tioga Road. (209-372-8427)

TUOLUMNE STORE

This seasonal store offers a surprisingly good selection of groceries, beer, wine, books, and basic camping supplies. Located just west of Tuolumne Campground.

Lodging

Tuolumne Meadows Lodge (travelyosemite.com) offers the only overnight lodging in Tuolumne Meadows. Its 69 canvas tent cabins, which sleep up to four, have wood stoves and candles, but no electricity. Two miles east of Tioga Pass is Tioga Pass Resort (tiogapassresort.com), which has ten rustic cabins and four motel-style rooms at 9,550 feet of elevation. Additional lodging is available in the town of Lee Vining. Visit jameskaiser.com for additional lodging info.

Activities

RANGER PROGRAMS

Free ranger-led walks, hikes, and campfire programs are offered throughout summer and into fall. Topics include wildlife, botany, history, geology, and astronomy. Check the *Yosemite Guide* for current schedules.

PARSONS LODGE

This rustic stone building, a 30-minute walk from the Lembert Dome parking area, offers free programs exploring Yosemite's natural and cultural history on weekends in July and August. Presenters include writers, researchers, park rangers, and adventurers. Check the *Yosemite Guide* for current schedules.

YOSEMITE MOUNTAINEERING SCHOOL

The Yosemite Mountaineering School offers rock climbing lessons for all abilities in and around Tuolumne Meadows (209-372-8344, travelyosemite.com).

Dining

★ TIOGA PASS RESORT $$$ (Brk, Lnch, Din)

More than a wayside restaurant, Tioga Pass Resort is a High Sierra institution, luring visitors with its great menu and cozy atmosphere. The food is high on quality, low on pretension, and full of 9,500-foot alpine charm. Located two miles east of Tioga Pass.

★ TUOLUMNE MEADOWS LODGE $$$ (Brk, Din)

Tuolumne Meadows Lodge offers the only sit-down dining experience in Tuolumne Meadows. Diners are seated in random groups at large tables, which means you'll get to know your neighbors. Located next to the front office at Tuolumne Meadows Lodge. Reservations are required for dinner. Box lunches are available if ordered the night before (209-372-8413).

WHOA NELI DELI $$$ (Brk, Lnch, Din)

Located in a Mobil gas station—yes, a Mobil gas station—this otherwise nondescript mini-mart serves shockingly good food. From fresh pizzas and sandwiches to buffalo meatloaf and fish tacos with mango salsa, the menu is eclectic and extensive. Located near the junction of Tioga Road and Highway 395 in Lee Vining (760-647-1088).

TUOLUMNE MEADOWS GRILL $$$ (Lnch, Din)

This take-out grill serves fast food staples like burgers, hot dogs, and chicken sandwiches. There are also a handful of salads and healthy options. It ain't gourmet, but it sure tastes good after several days in the backcountry. Located next to the Tuolumne Store.

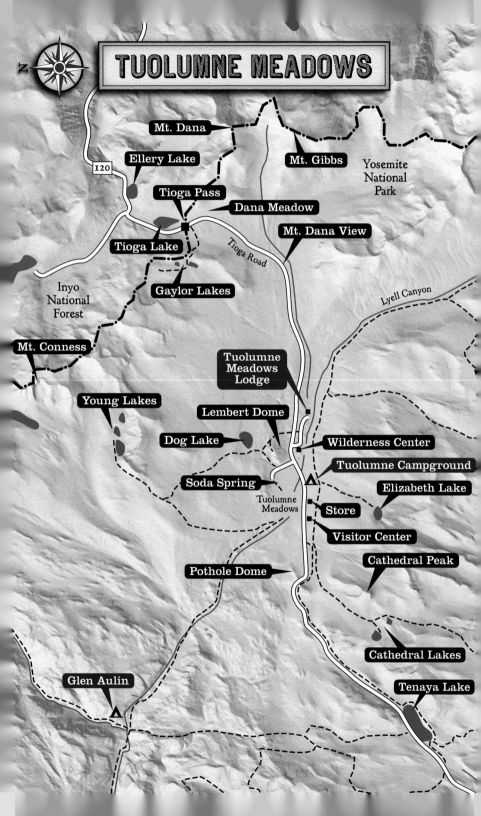

Pothole Dome

A 200-foot scramble to the top of this small dome offers great views of Tuolumne Meadows. Pothole Dome is named for a series of rounded depressions ("potholes") on its southern flank. The smooth granite surrounding the potholes is often mistaken for glacial polish—a glassy veneer created when the underside of a moving glacier buffs the bedrock to a shine—but the polish on Pothole Dome's southern flank was created by water, not ice. During the last Ice Age, water flowed *under* a glacier that covered Pothole Dome. The gritty water, channeled by a tunnel in the ice, flowed uphill over the dome, sculpting the potholes and polishing the rock. Actual glacial polish can be seen on Pothole Dome's eastern slope.

Soda Springs / Parsons Lodge

This naturally carbonated mineral spring isn't exactly picturesque, but good views of Tuolumne Meadows and the surrounding peaks make it a worthy destination. The path to Soda Springs is an easy 1.5-mile stroll—perfect for all ages. From the Lembert Dome parking area, follow the dirt road north and continue past the metal gate. The wooden cabin at Soda Springs was build by sheepherder John Baptiste Lembert around 1889. Just past the spring is Parsons Lodge (above), a rustic stone lodge built by the Sierra Club in 1915. For decades the building was used as a Sierra Club meeting house. Today Parsons Lodge houses interesting exhibits and hosts free natural history lectures on summer weekends.

Lembert Dome

Looming 900 feet over the eastern end of Tuolumne Meadows, Lembert Dome is named for John-Baptiste Lembert, a sheepherder who homesteaded in Tuolumne Meadows in the late 1800s. In a strange twist of fate, the geological term used to describe rock formations like Lembert Dome is *roche moutonnée* ("stone sheep"). Roche moutonnées form when a glacier flows over a large rock outcrop, smoothing out a gradual uphill slope. After rounding the peak, the glacier plucks away rocks on the downhill slope, forming a steep drop-off. A short trail heads to the top of Lembert Dome, which offers stunning 360-degree views of Tuolumne Meadows and the surrounding peaks (p.256).

Mt. Dana / Mt. Gibbs View

This roadside pullout along the Dana Fork of the Tuolumne River offers great views of Mt. Dana (on the left) and Mt. Gibbs. The pullout is marked by a small post labeled T36. At 13,053 feet Mt. Dana is the second-highest peak in the park. Only Mt. Lyell (13,114 feet) is taller. Mt. Gibbs (12,764 feet) is the fifth-highest peak in the park. While savoring the view of Mt. Dana and Mt. Gibbs, notice their dark coloration. The two peaks are composed of ancient metamorphic rocks that once covered all of Yosemite's granite. This is one of the few places in the park where these ancient metamorphic rocks remain visible. A strenuous 3-mile hike heads to the top of Mt. Dana (p.276).

Dana Meadow

This beautiful meadow, located just west of the park boundary, lies 1,000 feet higher than Tuolumne Meadows. Twenty thousand years ago both meadows were buried under a massive glacier. Then, when global temperatures warmed around 15,000 years ago, the ice started to melt. As the glacier retreated, huge chunks of ice broke off and formed depressions in the ground called *kettles*. The kettles filled with water, and the small ponds you see today are remnants of those ancient kettles. You may also notice dozens of fallen trees on the north side of the meadow. Can you guess why all the fallen trees point downhill? If you guessed avalanche, give yourself a prize.

Tioga Pass

At 9,941 feet, Tioga Pass (above) is the highest highway pass in California. It marks Yosemite's eastern boundary, which is also the watershed boundary for the Tuolumne River. Precipitation that falls west of Tioga Pass flows down the Tuolumne River en route to San Francisco. Precipitation that falls east of Tioga Pass flows down Lee Vining Creek towards Mono Lake and the Great Basin Desert. As Highway 120 heads east from Tioga Pass, it plunges down the sheer eastern slope of the Sierra Nevada Mountains to the small town of Lee Vining. Along the way you'll be treated to glorious views of Tioga Lake, Ellery Lake, and Lee Vining Canyon.

East of Tioga Pass, Tioga Road enters one of its most dramatic stretches. It starts innocently enough, twisting through pine forests and passing a pair of beautiful alpine lakes. Then, suddenly, Tioga Road makes a sharp turn into Lee Vining Canyon, a startling expanse that slices through the crest of the Sierra Nevada. Over the next nine miles, Tioga Road plummets over 2,000 feet. Whatever you lose in brake pads you'll gain in majestic scenery. (Tip: shift into low gear during the descent.) If you think driving the road is tough, try *running* up it. That's what over 100 masochists do each September during the Tioga Pass Run. The 12.4-mile race, which starts in Lee Vining and ends at Tioga Pass, climbs 3,200 feet. Top runners complete the race in under 90 minutes.

~ LEMBERT DOME ~

SUMMARY For a relatively quick Tuolumne hike with dramatic views, nothing beats Lembert Dome. Rising to a maximum elevation of 9,450 feet, Lembert Dome offers panoramic views of Tuolumne Meadows, the Cathedral Range, and the rugged peaks along the Sierra Nevada's eastern crest. From Dog Lake parking area the trail to Lembert Dome climbs through a forest, heads west at a junction, and emerges onto an open stretch of bare granite. At this point there's no official trail, but a series of cairns (small rock piles) guide hikers towards the summit. With broad views of the western horizon, Lembert Dome is a fantastic place to watch the sunset. If you do visit for sunset, be sure to bring a flashlight or headlight for the hike down.

TRAILHEAD The shortest and best route to the top of Lembert Dome starts from Dog Lake parking area near Tuolumne Lodge. Take the shuttle or drive east on Tioga Road from Tuolumne Meadows and turn right towards Tuolumne Lodge. Follow the road to the Dog Lake parking area. The trail starts at the upper end of the parking area and crosses Tioga Road.

TRAIL INFO

RATING Moderate

HIKING TIME 2–3 hours

DISTANCE 2.8 miles, round-trip

ELEVATION CHANGE 850 feet

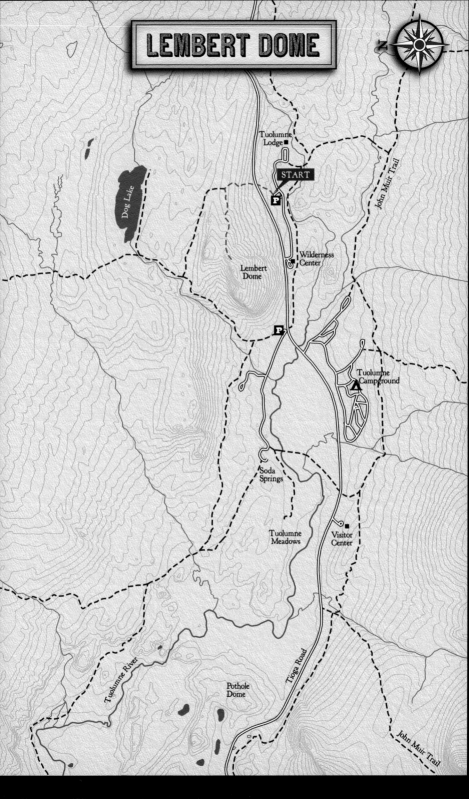

❧ CATHEDRAL LAKES ❧

SUMMARY These two small lakes, nestled along the John Muir Trail, are among the prettiest in Yosemite. Kick back on the smooth granite shores of Lower Cathedral Lake and revel in the dramatic views of Cathedral Peak. Or continue to the flower-strewn meadows surrounding Upper Cathedral Lake and check out Cathedral Peak from a different perspective. The hike to Cathedral Lakes is an uphill workout, but the gorgeous scenery is more than worth it. Lower Cathedral Lake, reached via a half-mile spur trail, is the larger of the two lakes. If you've got a limited amount of time or energy, spend it there. But if your inner lake lover is thirsting for more, continue half a mile past the spur trail to Upper Cathedral Lake. Backpacking note: Upper Cathedral Lake is a popular camping spot, but overnight camping is not allowed at Lower Cathedral Lake.

TRAILHEAD The trail to Cathedral Lakes starts about 1.5 miles west of the Tuolumne Visitor Center. Parking is often tight due to the trail's popularity. Consider parking at the nearby Tuolumne Meadows Visitors Center and walking half a mile to the trailhead.

TRAIL INFO

RATING Moderate

HIKING TIME 4–6 hours

DISTANCE 7.5 miles, round-trip

ELEVATION CHANGE 1,000 feet

⤳ ELIZABETH LAKE ⤳

SUMMARY While not as dramatic as Cathedral Lakes, Elizabeth Lake is a close runner-up, with lush meadows and shimmering reflections of granite peaks. The round-trip hike to Elizabeth Lake is also three miles shorter—perfect for lake lovers with a limited amount of time. Unicorn Peak towers above the lake's southern shore. The peak's "peculiar horn-shaped outline"—though hardly unicorn-esque from this angle—inspired the Whitney Survey to name it after the mythical creature. Experienced hikers can attempt a rugged scramble to the top of Unicorn Peak, which offers terrific 10,900-foot views of Tuolumne Meadows. Most visitors will be content to simply lounge around the lake. Following snowy winters, a long snow chute often lingers at the far end of the lake. Note: camping is not allowed at Elizabeth Lake.

TRAILHEAD The trail to Elizabeth Lake starts in the Tuolumne Campground near the group camp restrooms on the B Loop. Signs in the campground will direct you to the trailhead. Don't be put off by the initial steep climb—the trail quickly mellows out.

TRAIL INFO

RATING Moderate

DISTANCE 4.6 miles, round-trip

HIKING TIME 3–4 hours

ELEVATION CHANGE 850 feet

✑ GLEN AULIN ✎

SUMMARY Situated next to a gorgeous backcountry waterfall, Glen Aulin is one of Yosemite's most popular High Sierra Camps. The hike to Glen Aulin starts in Tuolumne Meadows and follows the cascading Tuolumne River almost entirely downhill. You'll have to hike uphill on the way back, but after a good night's sleep in a comfy tent cabin you'll be ready to hit the trail. Glen Aulin is also the jumping-off point for several longer backpacks, including the Grand Canyon of the Tuolumne (p.284) and Matterhorn Canyon (p.288). Due to Glen Aulin's popularity, a backpackers' campground with bear boxes and toilets is located behind the High Sierra Camp. To protect the water quality of the Tuolumne River drainage, which supplies San Francisco with drinking water, Glen Aulin's high-tech composting toilet was built at a cost of several hundred thousand dollars. So be sure to take advantage of this luxurious backcountry throne.

TRAILHEAD From the Lembert Dome parking area, follow the broad path towards Soda Springs and then follow the signs to Glen Aulin.

TRAIL INFO

RATING Moderate

DISTANCE 10.4 miles, round-trip

HIKING TIME 6–8 hours

ELEVATION CHANGE 800 feet

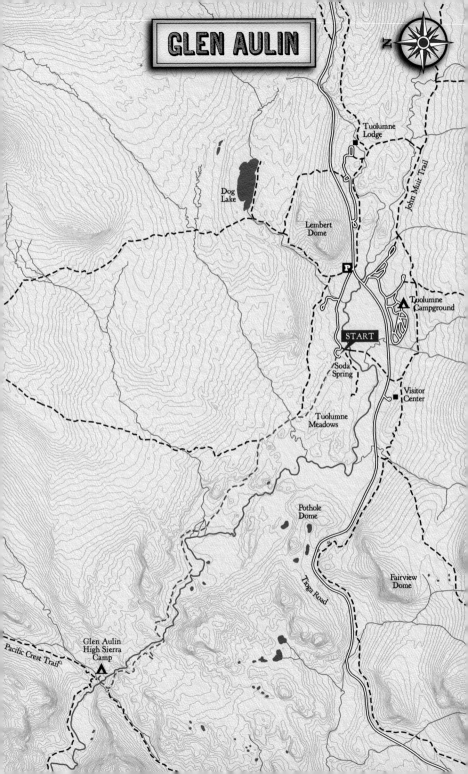

⊰ GAYLOR LAKES ⊱

SUMMARY This dramatic hike brings you to two shimmering lakes near the ruins of an old mining camp. Starting at an elevation of 10,000 feet, it's one of the highest day hikes in Yosemite—which means open scenery with terrific views of the surrounding High Sierra. The trail starts near the park's eastern boundary and climbs a steep ridge with great views of Dana Meadow. From there the trail descends to the first lake, skirting the northern shore as the jagged peaks of the Cathedral Range seem to rise above the water to the west. Continue to the upper lake and you'll find permanent snowfields lying in the shade of the mountains. After wrapping around the shore, the trail climbs a small ridge with sweeping views of both lakes. Nearby are the crumbling remains of the Great Sierra Mine, a failed silver-mining operation that was established here in the 1800s. Note: camping is not allowed at Gaylor Lakes.

TRAILHEAD The trail starts from the small parking area with a restroom just west of the Tioga Pass entrance station. You can also ride the shuttle, which stops at Gaylor Lakes trailhead.

TRAIL INFO

RATING Moderate

DISTANCE 5 miles, round-trip

HIKING TIME 2–3 hours

ELEVATION CHANGE 800 feet

⊸ YOUNG LAKES ⊷

SUMMARY These three picture-perfect lakes make a long, rewarding day hike or a terrific overnight backpack. Lower Young Lake, surrounded by lodgepole pines and dramatic granite, is distinguished by its sandy beaches. Middle Young Lake is the smallest of the three. Upper Young Lake, located above treeline, offers the most spectacular scenery. The shortest, most scenic route to Young Lakes heads towards Dog Lake and continues north. (Note: a less steep but longer route branches off the Glen Aulin trail about a mile past Soda Springs.) If you're spending at least two nights at Young Lakes, nearby Mt. Conness makes a spectacular day hike, but it's only suitable for rugged hikers used to off-trail travel. To climb Mt. Conness, head north from Middle or Upper Young Lake, skirt the ravine towards a series of marshy ponds, and pick up the unofficial use trail. Backpacking note: campfires are not allowed at Young Lakes.

TRAILHEAD The trailhead via Dog Lake starts near the picnic tables at the Lembert Dome parking area. The info listed below is for a hike to Lower Young Lake; Upper Young Lake is about 0.7 miles beyond Lower Young Lake.

◖ TRAIL INFO ◗

RATING Strenuous   **HIKING TIME** 8–10 hours

DISTANCE 13.5 miles, round-trip   **ELEVATION CHANGE** 1,500 feet

"The mighty Sierra, miles in height ... so gloriously colored and so radiant, it seemed not clothed with light but wholly composed of it, like the wall of some celestial city .... Then it seemed to me that the Sierra should be called, not the Nevada or Snowy Range, but the Range of Light."

— John Muir

Mount Conness (left) from Young Lakes

Hiking between Young Lakes & Mt. Conness

⊰ MOUNT CONNESS ⊱

SUMMARY At 12,590 feet, Mount Conness is the eighth-tallest peak in Yosemite, and the tallest peak in the Sierra Nevada north of Tioga Road. Its sheer southwest face—a favorite among rock climbers—is one of the High Sierra's most iconic sights. The summit of Mount Conness lies on the national park boundary. The most direct route to the top starts outside the park in the adjacent Inyo National Forest. From Sawmill Campground an unofficial trail climbs to Alpine Lake, then ascends to a wide plateau. The final push navigates a narrow knife edge sure to quicken the pulse of all but the most battle-hardened hikers. The reward: sweeping views of the Sierra Nevada, including Conness Glacier, the second-largest glacier in Yosemite after Lyell Glacier (p.56). Note: an easier but longer route to the top of Mount Conness starts from Young Lakes (p.266).

TRAILHEAD From Tioga Pass drive 2.1 miles north, then turn left onto Saddlebag Lake Road. Follow the dirt road 1.6 miles to Sawmill Campground. The trail starts from the northwest end of the campground.

TRAIL INFO

RATING Difficult

DISTANCE 8 miles, round-trip

HIKING TIME 6–8 hours

ELEVATION CHANGE 2,748 feet

View from Mt. Conness

～ෲ MOUNT DANA ୧～

SUMMARY At 13,053 feet, Mount Dana is the second-highest peak in the park after Mount Lyell (13,114 feet). And while Mount Lyell (p.56) requires a rugged, multi-day backpack and technical climbing, Mt. Dana can be summited in an afternoon. Perched on the Sierra Nevada's eastern crest, it offers 360-degree views of the High Sierra, Mono Lake, and the eastern deserts. The unofficial yet well-worn trail to the top starts at the Tioga Pass Entrance Station and climbs 1,700 feet to an open ridge. The final 1,000 feet requires a scamper up loose rocks. The final ascent can be confusing. Stay near the eastern edge and look for cairns (small rock piles) to guide you. Note: Mount Dana is often covered in snow well into the summer—ask about conditions before your hike. And if you see dark clouds approaching, do not attempt this hike. You do not want to be this high during one of the Sierra Nevada's legendary thunderstorms.

TRAILHEAD The trail to Mount Dana starts from the small parking area adjacent to the Tioga Pass Entrance Station. Ask the ranger at the kiosk for directions to the top, then follow the well-worn path east.

TRAIL INFO

RATING Very strenuous	**HIKING TIME** 5–6 hours
DISTANCE 5.8 miles, round-trip	**ELEVATION CHANGE** 3,100 feet

View from Mt. Dana

Mono Lake

This alkaline lake in the desert east of Yosemite is famous for tufa towers. These unusual calcium carbonate spires, formed at underwater springs, are currently exposed due to historically low lake levels.

In 1941 the city of Los Angeles extended its aqueduct system to divert water flowing into Mono Lake. The lake lost one-third of its surface area, and Negit Island, which was previously in the center of the lake, turned into a peninsula. The island was a critical nesting site for birds. Over 50,000 gulls, roughly 85% of California's breeding population, nest at Mono Lake. When the island became a peninsula, coyotes marched across to feast on bird eggs. In 1978 the Mono Lake Committee teamed up with the Audubon Society to restore Mono Lake. In 1994 the lake's tributary streams won legal protection, and the lake's levels have been slowly rising ever since. Today the lake covers roughly 70 square miles—about twice the size of San Francisco.

Twenty thousand years ago, in the depths of the Ice Age, Mono Lake was much larger. The surface of that ancient lake, called Lake Russell, lay at an elevation of 7,140 feet—nearly 750 feet higher than today. Glaciers descend-

ing from the eastern Sierra Nevada emptied directly into the lake, carving off icebergs into the water. As temperatures warmed, however, Mono Lake became smaller and smaller, and dissolved salts from runoff concentrated. Today nearly 300 million tons of salt are dissolved in Mono Lake, making it 2.5 times saltier than the ocean.

Mono Lake is too salty for fish, but trillions of brine shrimp inhabit the waters in the warm, summer months. The shrimp are an important food source for the roughly 2 million migratory birds that visit Mono Lake each year. The lake is also home to strange "scuba diving" alkali flies. Most flies avoid water because they can drown or become fish food. But in fish-free Mono Lake, the underwater world offers flies tasty algae and no predators. As a result, Mono Lake's alkali flies evolved unusually hairy, waxy bodies that trap air bubbles, allowing them to stay underwater for up to 15 minutes.

Mono Lake was named after the Mono tribe, who gathered alkali fly larvae along its shore. They considered crushed fly larvae a delicacy. As one white explorer noted in 1863, "The Indians gave me some; it does not taste bad, and if one were ignorant of its origin, it would make fine soup."

Mono Lake from Mt. Dana

⊸ VOGELSANG ᨒ

SUMMARY At 10,100 feet, Vogelsang is Yosemite's highest High Sierra Camp. While the other four High Sierra Camps are nestled among stately forests, Vogelsang is located above treeline, providing terrific views of the surrounding peaks. If you find yourself enthralled by Yosemite's granite landscapes, this is the High Sierra Camp for you. In addition to grand views, there's a gurgling creek flowing through lush meadows—a great place to bask in Sierra sunshine. Five hundred feet above the High Sierra Camp lies gorgeous Vogelsang Lake, nestled in a granite bowl between Vogelsang Peak (11,516) and Fletcher Peak (11,410). Backpackers heading to Vogelsang should consider hiking the 19-mile loop that passes Evelyn Lake and heads back to the trailhead via Lyell Canyon—one of the finest three-day backpacks in the park.

TRAILHEAD The trail to Vogelsang starts from the parking area at Tuolumne Lodge. The lodge parking area is for guests only, so park in the nearby Dog Lake parking area or ride the shuttle. Follow the John Muir Trail about a mile to Rafferty Creek, then head towards Vogelsang.

TRAIL INFO

RATING Strenuous

HIKING TIME 7–8 hours

DISTANCE 13.6 miles, round-trip

ELEVATION CHANGE 1,500 feet

⊰ GRAND CANYON ᵒᶠ the TUOLUMNE ᏽ

SUMMARY This rugged backpack descends 4,700 feet down the stunning Grand Canyon of the Tuolumne River, then climbs 3,600 feet up to White Wolf Lodge. It's one of the most physically demanding backpacks in the park, but the scenic rewards are unparalleled. In places, the Grand Canyon of the Tuolumne rivals Arizona's Grand Canyon in depth. As you descend the Grand Canyon of the Tuolumne, you'll be treated to dozens of roaring cascades. The most famous is Waterwheel Falls, where the river glides down smooth granite slopes, then explodes into a series of huge rooster-tail arcs. The trail continues below 5,000 feet in elevation, where black oaks and chaparral are common. (Watch out for rattlesnakes!) Spend the night in Pate Valley—and rest up for the next day's grueling ascent. Upon reaching White Wolf Lodge, you'll be ready for a hot shower, a tasty meal, and a cozy bed. Book a night at White Wolf Lodge before your trip and finish off the hike in style.

TRAILHEAD Hike down to Glen Aulin (p.262) from Tuolumne Meadows. From Glen Aulin continue following the Tuolumne River downhill.

TRAIL INFO

RATING Very strenuous

DISTANCE 28 miles, one-way

HIKING TIME 2–3 days

ELEVATION CHANGE 4,700 feet

GRAND CANYON OF THE TUOLUMNE

N

Tuolumne
Meadows

START

Glen Aulin
High Sierra Camp

Sunrise
High Sierra Camp

Tenaya
Lake

Waterwheel
Falls

May Lake
High Sierra Camp

Ten Lakes

Muir
Gorge

Porcupine
Flat

Tioga Road

Pate
Valley

Yosemite
Creek

White
Wolf

Hetch Hetchy
Reservoir

"For miles the river is one wild, exulting, on-rushing mass ... gliding in magnificent silver plumes, dashing and foaming through huge boulder-dams, leaping high into the air in wheel-like whirls ... singing in exuberance of mountain energy."

—John Muir

Waterwheel Falls

⚜ MATTERHORN CANYON ⚜

SUMMARY   Lying in the remote northeast corner of Yosemite, Matterhorn Canyon is one of the park's most spectacular and least-visited places. Getting here requires several days of backpacking through rugged wilderness. But for quint-essential High Sierra splendor—snow-capped peaks, flowery meadows, glacially carved U-shaped valleys—few hikes in the Sierra Nevada compare. After follow-ing the Pacific Crest Trail for 20 miles from Tuolumne Meadows, you'll head north into Matterhorn Canyon. The jagged Sawtooth Range looms above as you ascend to Burro Pass (10,600 feet). After savoring the dramatic views, drop down into the meadowy, boulder-strewn canyon that heads to Mule Pass (10,400 feet). Say goodbye to Yosemite as you enter the Hoover Wilderness, which treats you to a handful of idyllic lakes before the hike ends at bustling Twin Lakes.

TRAILHEAD   From Tuolumne Meadows head to Glen Aulin (p.262), then follow the Pacific Crest Trail through Cold Canyon. Note: this one-way trip ends at Twin Lakes, where you can leave your car for several days for a small fee.

◆ TRAIL INFO ◆

RATING Very strenuous   **HIKING TIME** 6–8 days

DISTANCE 38.4 miles, round-trip   **ELEVATION CHANGE** 3,500 feet

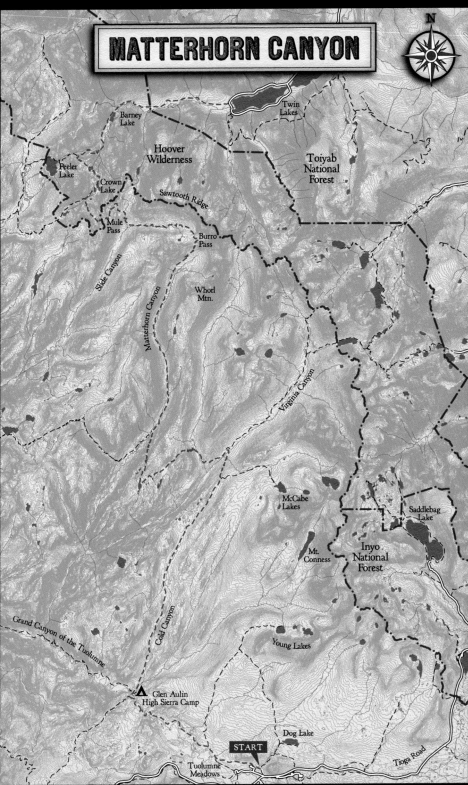

Matterhorn Canyon

U–Shaped Valleys

Matterhorn Canyon and the surrounding High Sierra offer some of the best examples of U-shaped valleys in Yosemite. Prior to the Ice Age, the Sierra Nevada was filled with steep, V-shaped valleys cut by tumbling streams over millions of years. During the depths of the Ice Age, massive glaciers flowed through the V-shaped valleys, gouging out their sides and leaving graceful, U-shaped valleys in their wake. But the highest peaks (including the Sawtooth Range, above) remained above the flowing ice and kept their jagged profiles.

WAWONA

LOCATED AT THE southernmost tip of Yosemite, Wawona lacks the bold drama found in much of the park. There are no sheer cliffs or thousand-foot waterfalls, just a quiet meadow and stream surrounded by forest. But Wawona is noteworthy for its proximity to the Mariposa Grove of giant sequoias, and there are plenty of additional activities that make it a worthy destination.

The Mariposa Grove, located just east of South Entrance Station, is the largest giant sequoia grove in Yosemite. Among its 500-plus specimens is Grizzly Giant, the largest tree in the park. About six miles northwest of the Mariposa Grove lies Wawona Hotel and the Pioneer History Center. Adjacent to the hotel is the Wawona Visitor Center at Hill's Studio (209-375-9531), where a knowledgeable staff answers questions, issues wilderness permits, and sells books and maps. Just north of the hotel is the Wawona Store, which sells groceries and other supplies, plus a post office and a 24-hour gas station. There's no gas in Yosemite Valley (25 miles distant) so if you're heading that way it's a good idea to fill up here. One mile northwest of the gas station is Wawona Campground, which hosts free ranger campfire programs on weekends. Nature walks and evening programs are also offered during the week (check the *Yosemite Guide* for current schedules).

Native tribes once lived near present-day Wawona along the banks of the South Fork of the Merced River, an area they call *Pallachun* ("Good Place to Stop"). In autumn, when the river ran low, they dumped crushed soaproot in the water. According to Galen Clark (p.98), who moved to the area in 1856, the soaproot "roiled the water and made it somewhat foamy. The fish were soon affected by it, became stupid with a sort of strangulation, and rose to the surface, where they were easily captured by the Indians with their scoop baskets."

Shortly after moving here, Galen Clark opened a small hotel catering to tourists on their way to Yosemite Valley. It was said that of all the supplies delivered to Clark's Station, cases of wine, whiskey, and brandy far outnumbered cases of food. Clark was a popular host but a lousy businessman, and in 1874 he sold his hotel to the Washburn brothers. In 1879 they built the current hotel, and in 1882 they renamed the area "Wawona" after the supposed native word for giant sequoias. *Wawona* is an imitation of a hooting owl, which is considered the guardian spirit of the big trees.

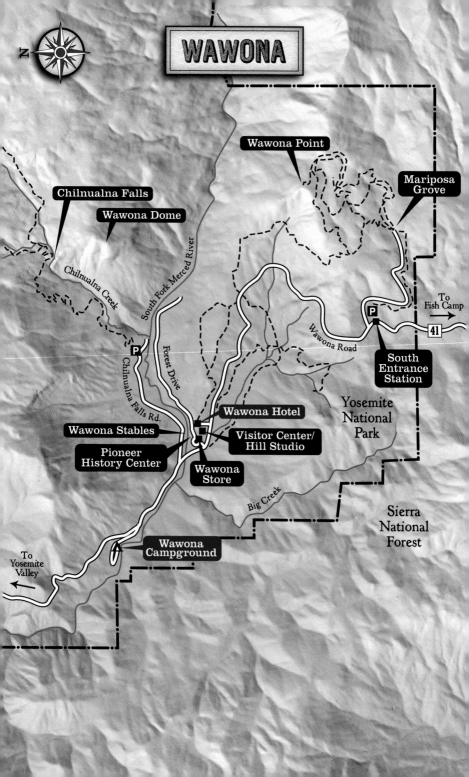

Wawona Hotel

Built in 1879, the Wawona Hotel is filled with Victorian-era charm. Even if you're not a guest, you can eat in the elegant dining room (209-375-1425) or enjoy a drink in the lobby/lounge, where local musician Tom Bopp often plays piano. Saturday barbecues on the lawn are a summer treat, as well as evening cocktails on the front porch. The hotel's Golf Shop (209-375-6572) rents equipment and organizes tee times on the adjacent nine-hole golf course. Notice the fountain in front of the hotel. In 1888 a popular guidebook depicted the Wawona Hotel with a dramatic fountain in front, despite the fact that no fountain existed. So many guests complained about the missing fountain that the owners installed one—and it continues to greet visitors to this day.

Thomas Hill Studio

This small building, located just west of Wawona Hotel, was the former studio of artist Thomas Hill. From 1885 until his death in 1908, Hill used this studio to paint acclaimed landscapes of Yosemite. Today the building functions as a visitor center, gift shop, and mini-exhibition space.

Pioneer History Center

There's no better place to explore Yosemite's pioneer past than this small cluster of historic buildings, which were relocated here from other parts of the park. There are log cabins, a jail, a Wells Fargo office, a blacksmith shop, a covered bridge (one of only half a dozen in California), and a collection of vintage stagecoaches. Walk across the covered bridge to the main square and look for signs listing seasonal activities, including blacksmith demonstrations and ten-minute horse-drawn stage rides ($5 adults, $4 kids).

Wawona Stables

Wawona Stables offers both horse and mule rides. Two-hour rides ($70) loop around Wawona Meadow. All-day rides ($144) visit the Mariposa Grove of giant sequoias. Riders must be at least 7 years old and 52 inches tall and must weigh less than 225 pounds. (travelyosemite.com)

Chilnualna Falls

This beautiful waterfall, reached via a strenuous trail that rises 2,400 feet in 4.1 miles, is one of Wawona's most rewarding hikes. The trailhead is located next to a parking area 1.7 miles from the start of Chilnualna Falls Road.

Mariposa Grove

Home to the largest collection of giant sequoias (p.72) in the park, Mariposa Grove is one of the highlights of Yosemite. Over ten miles of hiking trails twist through the 250-acre grove, passing over 500 massive trees.

In 1864 Abraham Lincoln signed the Yosemite Grant, which protected both Yosemite Valley and Mariposa Grove. It was the first time in history a government protected land for future generations simply because it was beautiful. The Yosemite Grant laid the foundation for the creation of national parks—an idea born in America that ultimately spread around the world.

Start your visit at the Mariposa Grove Welcome Plaza, where a free shuttle takes visitors to Mariposa Grove. From the shuttle drop-off follow Big Trees Loop to Fallen Monarch, an enormous sequoia, 15 feet in diameter, that toppled over centuries ago.

From Fallen Monarch continue 0.5 miles to Grizzly Giant. Over 200 feet tall with a 30-foot base, Grizzly Giant is roughly 3,000 years old. One of its branches is over six feet in diameter—larger than most trees east of the Mississippi.

Just north of Grizzly Giant lies the California Tunnel Tree, where you can walk through a tunnel cut into the base of the tree. (The tunnel was cut in 1895, before such behavior was considered irresponsible.) From the California Tunnel Tree you can head back to the shuttle stop along Grizzly Giant Loop, or continue to the upper grove, where you'll enjoy hundreds of big trees with limited crowds. Highlights of the upper grove include: Mariposa Grove Cabin, a reconstruction of the cabin where Galen Clark (p.98) once lived; Telescope Tree, where you can stand inside the hollowed-out center and gaze up to the sky; and Wawona Point, which offers sweeping views of the surrounding landscape.

Trails along the perimeter of Mariposa Grove are open to horses. Yosemite Trails (yosemitetrails.com) offers guided horseback rides. In winter Mariposa Grove is open to snowshoers and cross-country skiers.

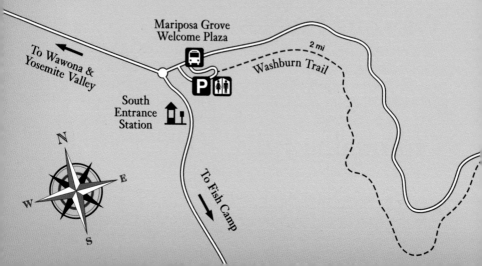

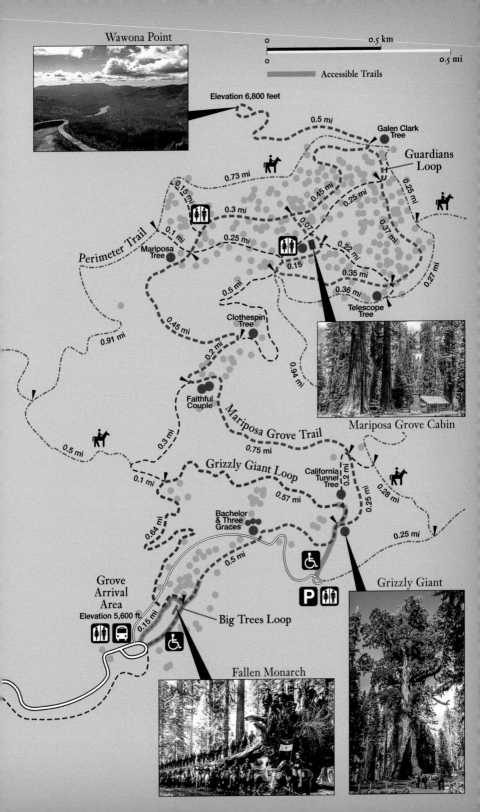

Wawona Point

0.5 km

0.5 mi

Accessible Trails

Elevation 6,800 feet

Galen Clark Tree

Guardians Loop

0.5 mi

0.73 mi

0.15 mi

0.45 mi

0.25 mi

0.3 mi

0.25 mi

0.25 mi

0.07

Perimeter Trail

0.1 mi

0.37 mi

Mariposa Tree

0.25 mi

0.22 mi

0.27 mi

0.15

0.35 mi

0.5 mi

0.36 mi

Telescope Tree

0.45 mi

Clothespin Tree

0.91 mi

0.2 mi

0.94 mi

Mariposa Grove Cabin

Faithful Couple

Mariposa Grove Trail

0.3 mi

Grizzly Giant Loop

0.75 mi

0.2 mi

0.5 mi

0.1 mi

California Tunnel Tree

0.28 mi

0.57 mi

0.25 mi

0.64 mi

0.25 mi

Bachelor & Three Graces

0.5 mi

Grove Arrival Area

Elevation 5,600 ft.

0.15 mi

Big Trees Loop

Grizzly Giant

Fallen Monarch

HETCH HETCHY

LOCATED ROUGHLY 12 miles northeast of Yosemite's Big Oak Flat Entrance—40 miles from Yosemite Valley—Hetch Hetchy is well off the beaten path. If you're visiting Yosemite for the first time, you'll probably want to spend your time elsewhere. But if you're fascinated by the reservoir's tumultuous environmental history (p.108), Hetch Hetchy and its waterfalls are worth a look.

Today Hetch Hetchy is an 8-mile long, 117-billion-gallon reservoir. Each day 220 million gallons of Hetch Hetchy water flow to nearly three million consumers in the San Francisco Bay Area. The water, which flows downhill along a 167-mile aqueduct, is so pure that it's usually exempted from federal water filtration requirements. And hydropower from O'Shaughnessy Dam generates 1.7 billion kilowatt-hours annually—enough to power 325,000 homes.

Before the dam was completed in 1923, Hetch Hetchy was a beautiful valley that many considered comparable to Yosemite Valley. The first white man to visit Hetch Hetchy was Nathan Screech, who arrived in the 1850s. Screech encountered several natives cooking a plant called *hatchhatchie*, and the word, later anglicized to "Hetch Hetchy," became the name of the valley.

When San Francisco politicians proposed flooding Hetch Hetchy in the early 1900s, John Muir and the Sierra Club fought back. Teddy Roosevelt twice vetoed legislation to build the dam, but in 1913 Woodrow Wilson signed the Raker Act, which authorized construction of the dam. In 1987 Interior Secretary Donald Hodel suggested removing the dam and restoring Hetch Hetchy Valley. Hodel's plan was opposed by California Congresswoman Nancy Pelosi and San Francisco Mayor Dianne Feinstein, who called the plan the worst idea to come from the Reagan administration since the sale of arms to Iran.

In 1999 the nonprofit group Restore Hetch Hetchy was founded, and in 2006 California's Department of Water Resources released a report that found "no fatal flaws in the restoration concept that would preclude additional study." Cost estimates of removing the dam range anywhere from one billion to ten billion dollars.

Hetch Hetchy is only open during daylight hours. To get there, exit Yosemite via the Big Oak Flat Entrance, drive one mile, and turn right onto Evergreen Road. Continue roughly seven miles to Mather Campground, then turn right towards the Hetch Hetchy Entrance Station. From the entrance it's about eight miles to Hetch Hetchy. There's a parking area next to the dam, and an easy 2.5-mile trail skirts the reservoir's northern shore en route to Tueeulala and Wapama Falls. The trail starts at the large tunnel next to the dam.

Extraordinary Parks
Extraordinary Guides

jameskaiser.com